Contents

W9-BEZ-199

Sharpen Your Skills—Reading • EMC 9718 • © Evan-Moor Corp.

Any Ants?

1 ant

2 ants

ants in
my pants

Aa

Listen for the Sound

Color the pictures that begin like ant.

Aa

Big or Little?

Draw 3 **big** things here.

Draw 3 **little** things here.

Seeing Shapes

Color the ○ ▬▬▬ .
Color the △ ▬▬▬ .
Color the □ ▬▬▬ .

What Color Is It?

a red car

It's red.

a blue cup

It's blue.

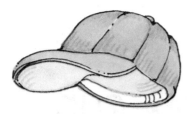

a green cap

It's green.

a yellow cat

It's yellow.

What Does It Say?

Draw a picture to show what the word says.

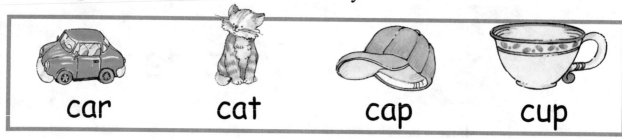

car   cat   cap   cup

car

cat

cap

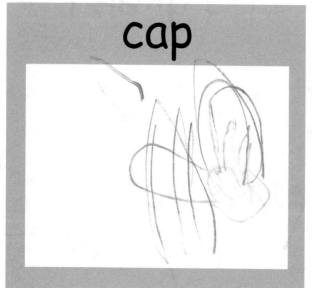

cup

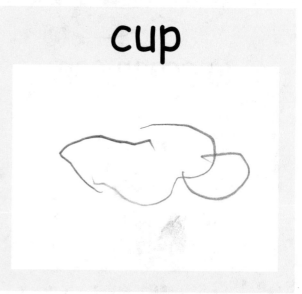

Cc

14

In the Cage

Connect the dots to finish the cage. Start with 1.

C c

Digging

excavar

Dig, Dog, dig.

Dig, Dog, dig.

después

After You Read

Practice the story.
Read it to an adult.

Dd

Sharpen Your Skills—Reading • EMC 9718 • © Evan-Moor Corp.

Listen for the Sound

Color the pictures that begin with the same sound as <u>dog</u>.

Dd

What Does It Say?

Draw a line from each name to the correct animal.

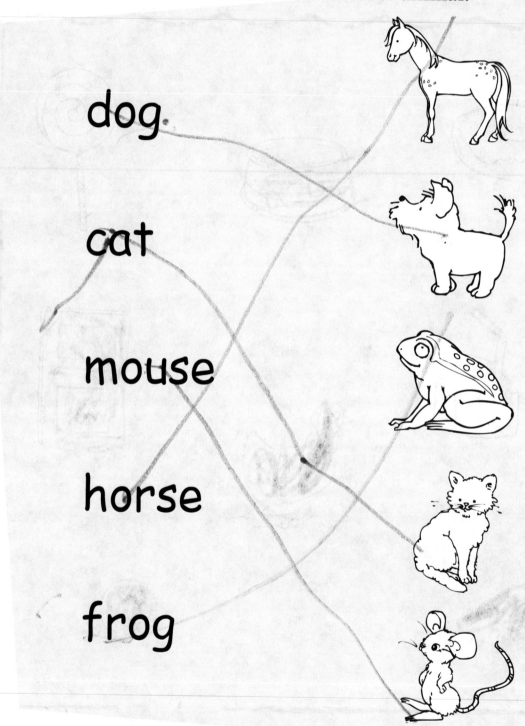

dog

cat

mouse

horse

frog

Dd

Dudley Duck

Trace the – – – – lines. Color the picture.

Trace and write.

duck duck duck

Dd

A Good Place to Dig

Fill in ◯ yes or ◯ no.

This is a good place to dig.
 yes no

This is a good place to dig.
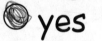 yes no

This is a good place to dig.
◯ yes ◯ no

This is a good place to dig.
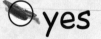 yes no

Dd

big eggs

little eggs

pretty eggs

Ee

Listen for the Sound

Color the pictures that begin with the same sound as egg.
Make an **X** on the pictures that begin with a different sound.

Ee

Sharpen Your Skills—Reading • EMC 9718 • © Evan-Moor Corp.

Seeing Words

Circle the words that are the same as the first word in each row.

egg	egg	eagle	egg
big	dig	big	big
little	little	little	lift
candy	dandy	candy	candy
good	good	dog	good

Ee

What Does It Say?

Circle the word that names the picture.

	ball	rug *manta*
	pen	cat
	egg	leg *pierna*
	book	ant
	dog	moon
	sun	cap

Ee

Is It Real?

es real

Fill in ⚪ yes or ⚪ no.

Is it real?
⚪ **yes**   ⚪ **no**

Is it real?
⚪ **yes**   ⚪ **no**

Is it real?
⚪ **yes**   ⚪ **no**

Is it real?
⚪ **yes**   ⚪ **no**

Ee

Swim, Fish, Swim

Little fish, little fish,
Swish, swish, swish.

Listen for the Sound

Cut and glue to show which pictures
begin with the same sound as fish.

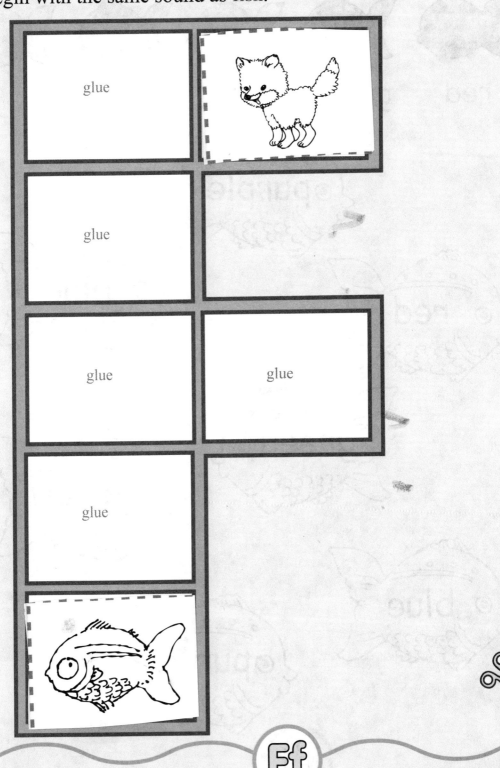

Ff

What Does It Say?

Color the fish.

red   green   blue   purple   yellow

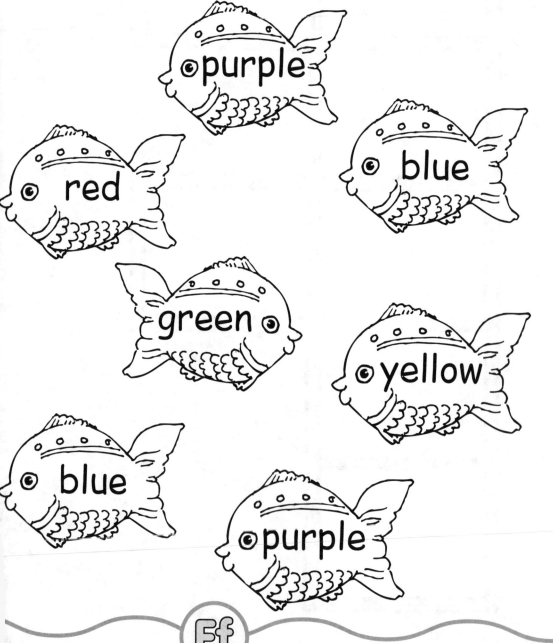

Ff

Rhyme Time

Circle the pictures in each line that rhyme.

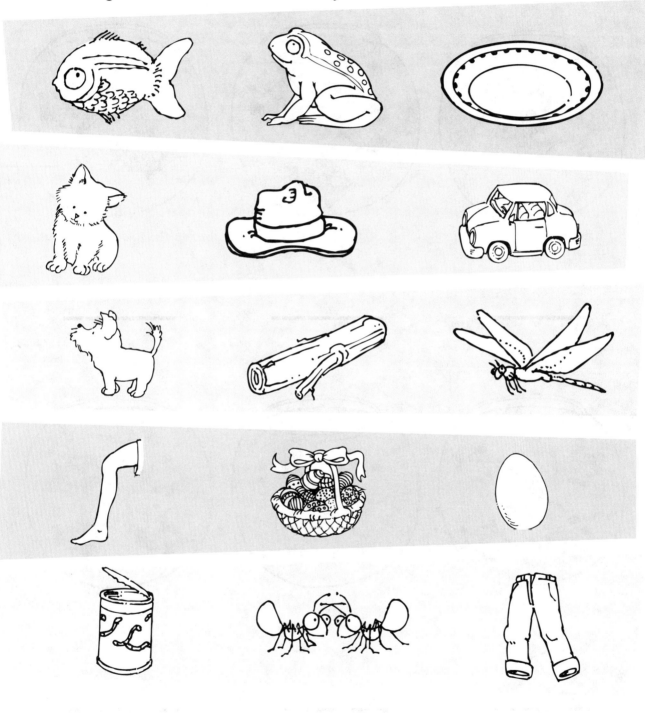

Ff

How Many?

Count. Write the number to tell how many.

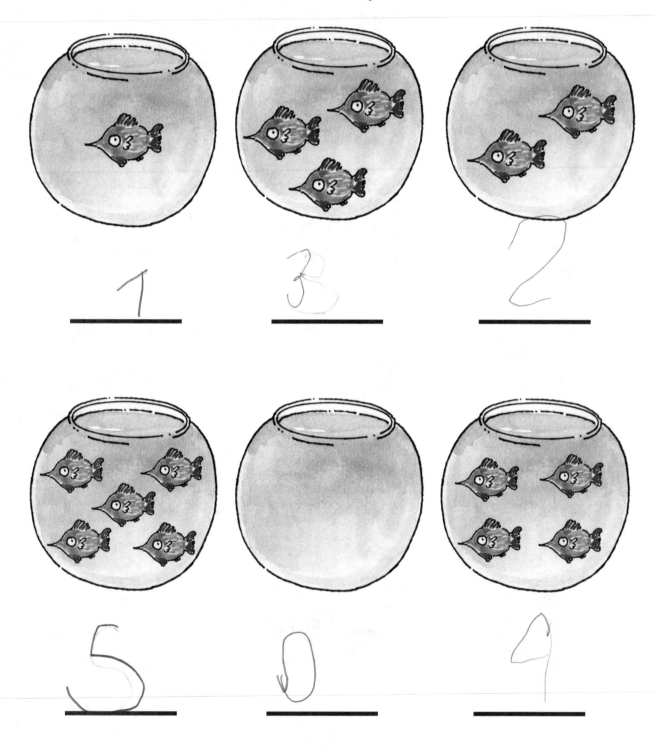

Good and Bad

Good!

Bad!

Good!

Bad!

What a day I had!

Listen for the Sound

Color the pictures that begin with the same sound as goat.

Gg

Sharpen Your Skills—Reading • EMC 9718 • © Evan-Moor Corp.

Put It in Order

Color, cut, and glue. Put the pictures in order.

1 glue	**2** glue
3 glue	**4** glue

Gg

G at the End

Circle the pictures that have the same ending sound as bag.

Gg

What Do You Think?

Trace.

Write good or bad.

Hippo's Hat

one hat
one big hat
one big red hat

Hh

Listen for the Sound

Circle the pictures that begin with the same sound as hippo.

H h

What Does It Say?

Draw a picture to show what each word means.

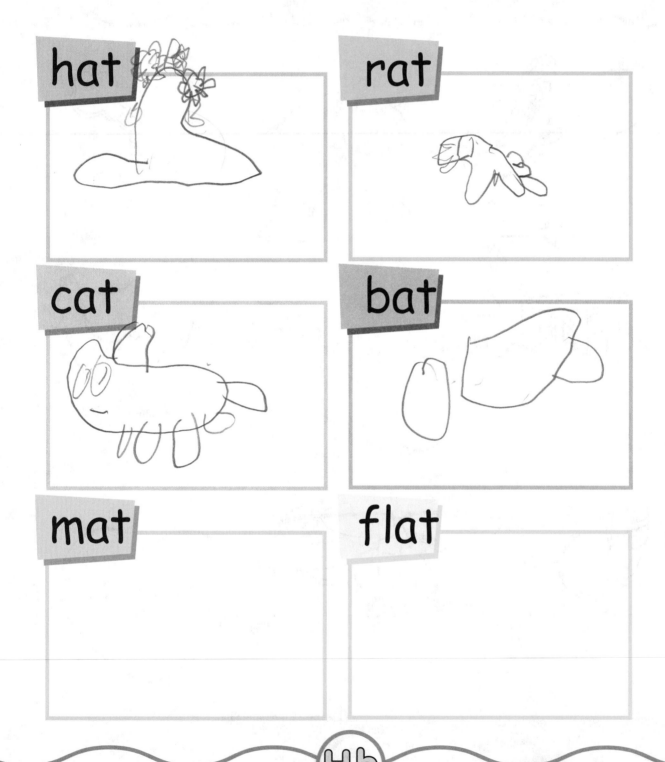

hat

rat

cat

bat

mat

flat

Hh

The House on the Hill

Follow the dots to make a hill.
Color the hill.
Draw a house on top.

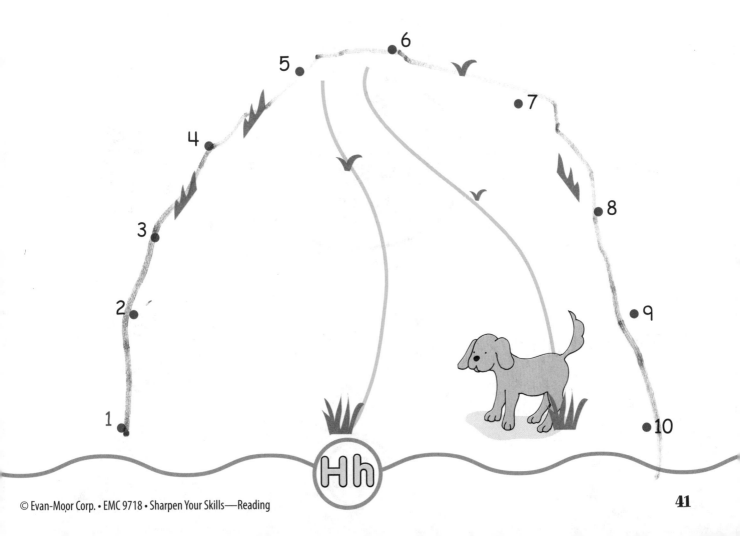

41

Is He Happy?

Fill in ◯ yes or ◯ no.

Is he happy?  ◯ yes ◯ no

Is he happy?  ◯ yes ◯ no

Is he happy?  ◯ yes ◯ no

Is he happy?  ◯ yes ◯ no

Hh

What's Inside?

Lift the lid.
See what hid.

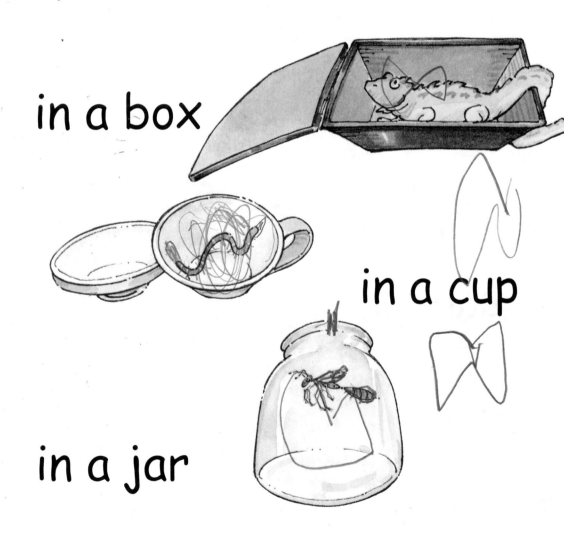

in a box

in a cup

in a jar

Close it up!

Ii

What Can You Do?

Read the words. Draw a picture to show what they say.

I can stop.

I can go.

Ii

Interesting Insects!

Color, cut, and glue. Put the insects in the jar.

My Insect Zoo

| glue | glue |
| glue | glue |

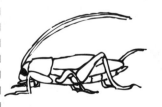

Ii

© Evan-Moor Corp. • EMC 9718 • Sharpen Your Skills—Reading

In or Out?

Where is it? Fill in ◯ **in** or ◯ **out**.

◯ in
◯ out

◯ in
◯ out

◯ in
◯ out

◯ in
◯ out

◯ in
◯ out

◯ in
◯ out

Ii

Find the Words

Circle the words that are the same in each row.

| big | big | dig | big |

| pig | dig | pig | pig |

| wig | wig | wig | mig |

| kick | lick | kick | kick |

| sick | sick | slick | sick |

| hill | hall | hill | hill |

Ii

Just a Jar

What's in the jar?

jam

What's in the jar?

jelly beans

What's in the jar?

June bug

After You Read

Practice the story.
Make it sound like you
are asking questions.
Read it to an adult.

Jj

Sharpen Your Skills—Reading • EMC 9718 • © Evan-Moor Corp.

Listen for the Sound

Cut and glue the pictures that begin
with the same sound as jar.

glue

glue

glue

glue

glue

What Does It Say?

Match each word to a picture. Color the pictures.

jar

jam

jet

jeep

Jj

How Many Balls?

Color. Count. Write the number word to tell how many.

<u>three</u> balls

_____ balls

_____ balls

_____ ball

Word Box

one   two   three   four   five   six

Jj

Just Jack

Color each puzzle piece that has a dot.

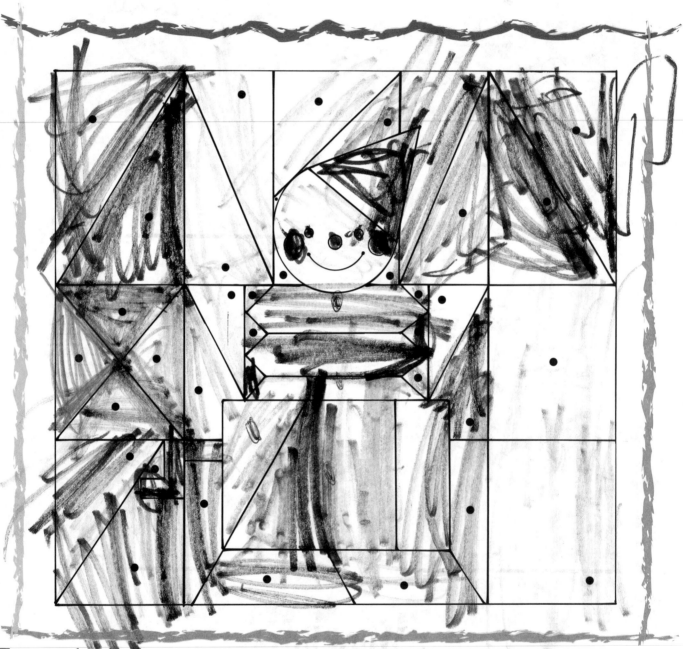

Trace and write.

Jj

Lock it up!

a key for the suitcase

Lock it up!

a key for the door

Start it up!

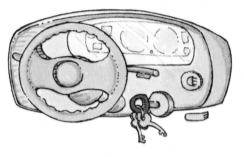

a key for the car

Here we go!

 Kk

Listen for the Sound

Circle the pictures that begin with the same sound as key.

Kk

Sharpen Your Skills—Reading • EMC 9718 • © Evan-Moor Corp.

Kites, Kites, Kites

Read the color words. Color the kites.

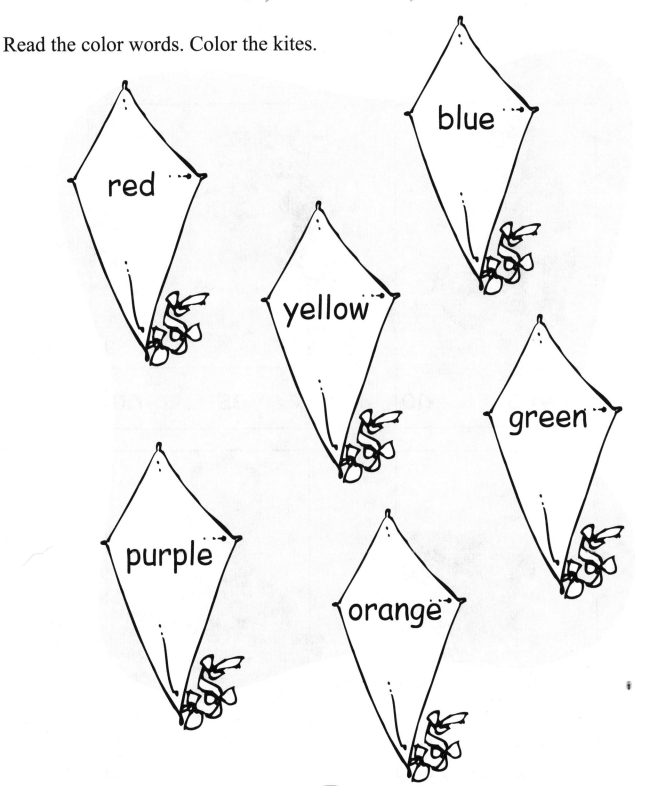

red

blue

yellow

green

purple

orange

Kk

Kindergarten

Could it happen in kindergarten? Fill in ◯ yes or ◯ no.

◯ yes ◯ no

◯ yes ◯ no

◯ yes ◯ no

◯ yes ◯ no

Kk

New Words

The pictures show what each new **k** word means. Draw a line to show who would use each thing.

kennel

kerchief

kettle

kayak

Let's Go to the Zoo

Look!

a lion

a llama

a leopard

a lollipop

Ll

Listen for the Sound

Say the name of each picture. Do you hear the l sound first or last?
Fill in ◯ first or ◯ last.

 ◯ first ◯ last

 ◯ first ◯ last

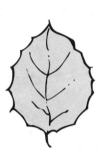 ◯ first ◯ last

 ◯ first ◯ last

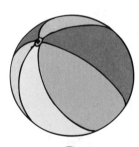 ◯ first ◯ last

 ◯ first ◯ last

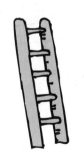 ◯ first ◯ last

 ◯ first ◯ last

 ◯ first ◯ last

Ll

Little or Large?

Color the pictures. Make an **X** on the little one.

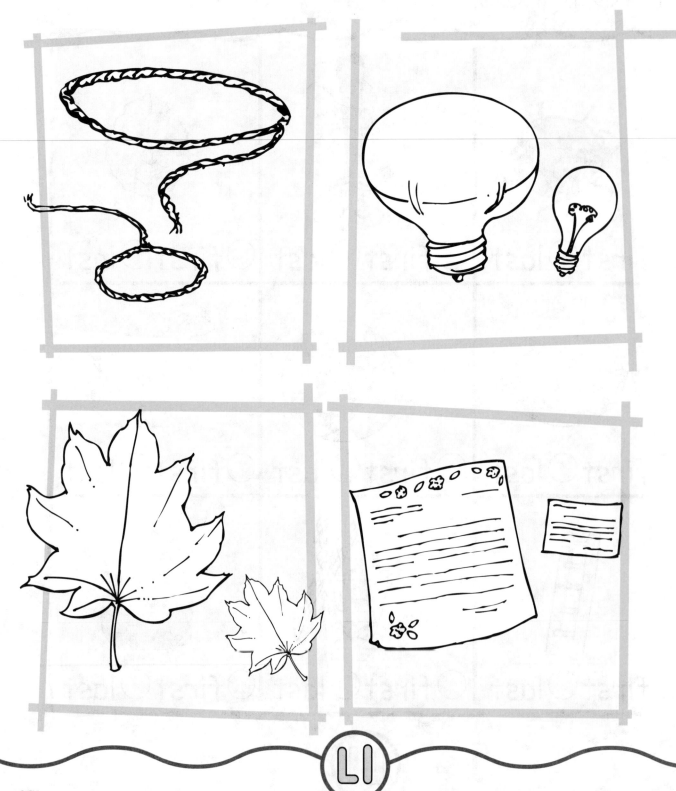

Ll

Look!
I can make new words!

Start with look.   l o o k

Take off the l.
Write a b.   __ o o k

Take off the b.
Write an h.   __ o o k

Take off the h.
Write a c   __ o o k

Take off the c.
Write br.   __ __ o o k

Ll

What's for Lunch?

Color the pictures that show food.

LI

Special Places

Little mouse has a house.

Little mole has a hole.

Little me in a tepee.

Mm

Listen for the Sound

Color the pictures that begin with the same sound as mouse.

Mail

Mm

Match the Mittens

Cut and glue to make pairs.

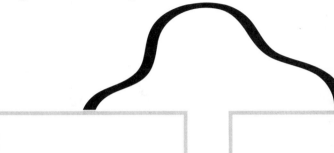

glue	glue

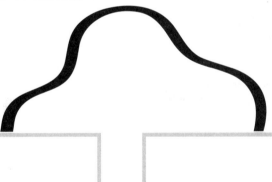

glue	glue

Mm

Where Am I?

Draw a line to make a match.

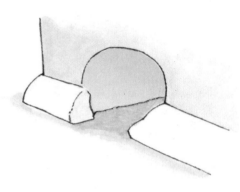

Find my house.

Find my tepee.

Find my hole.

Mm

In the Night Sky

Connect the dots. Start with **1**. Color the picture.

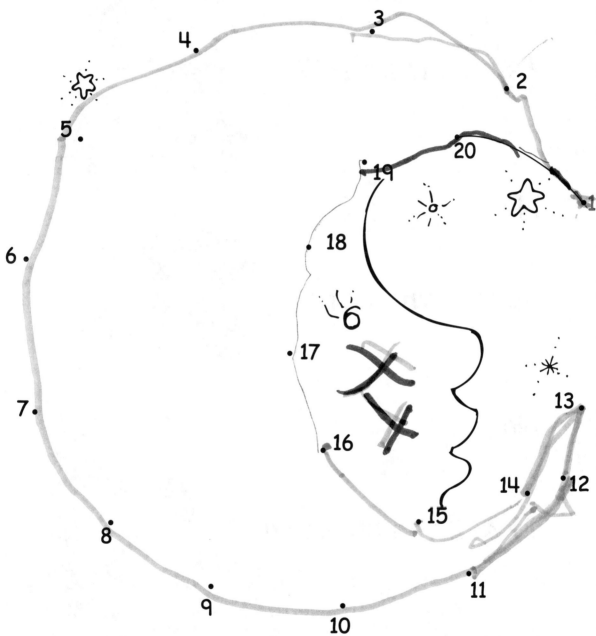

Have you ever seen the moon?

○ yes   ○ no

The New One

Is it in the nest?

No

Is it in the net?

No

It's in the nursery!

Yes!

Sharpen Your Skills—Reading • EMC 9718 • © Evan-Moor Corp.

Listen for the Sound

Cut and glue the pictures that begin with the same sound as net.

glue	glue
	glue
glue	glue

Nn

No, No, No

Write yes or no.

 The ball is red. _____

 The ball is green. _____

 The ball is yellow. _____

 The ball is brown. _____

Do you have a ball? _____

Do you play with a ball? _____

Noodle Necklace

Cut and glue. Make a necklace.

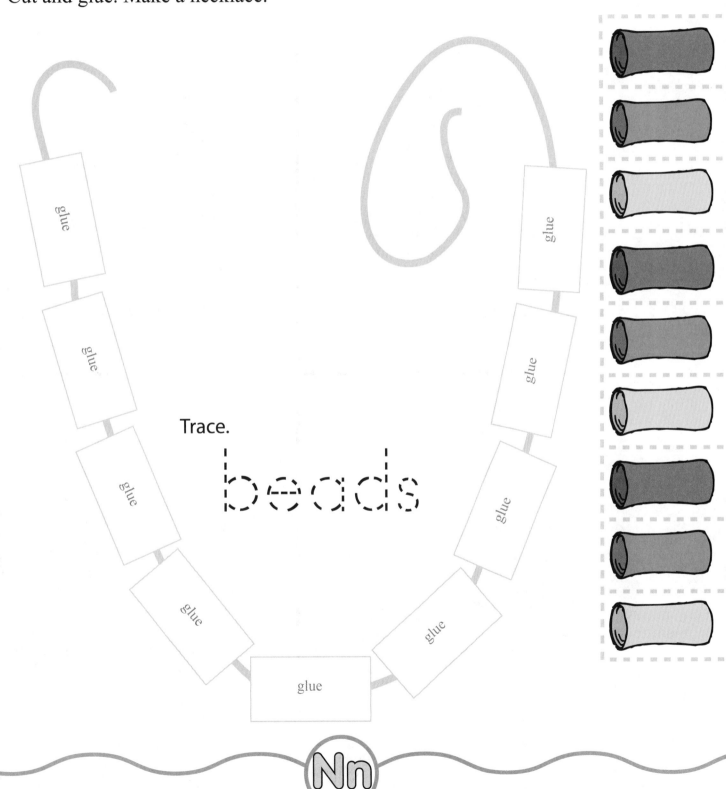

Trace.

beads

glue

glue

glue

glue

glue

glue

glue

glue

glue

Nn

Naughty or Nice?

Circle the word to tell whether they are naughty or nice.

○ naughty   ○ nice

○ naughty   ○ nice

○ naughty   ○ nice

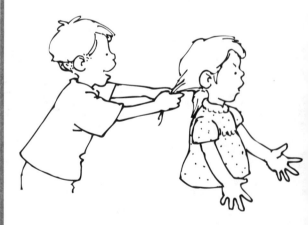

○ naughty   ○ nice

Where Do They Live?

This is an otter.
It lives in the water.

This is an ostrich.
It lives on the land.

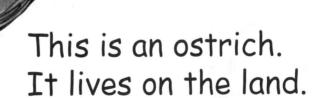

Listen for the Sound

Color the pictures that begin with the same sound as otter.

Making New Words

Add a letter to **–and** to make a new word that tells what the picture is.

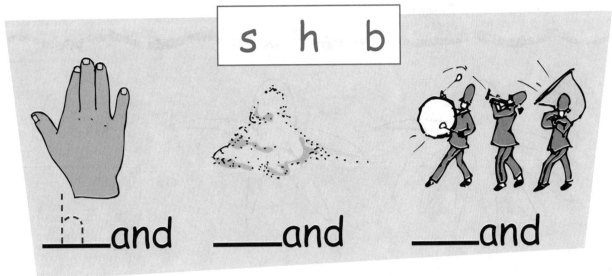

s h b

__h__and   ___and   ___and

Write one of the new words in each sentence.

Dump  the ___sand___.

Wash  your _____.

Hear  the _____.

Make Them Look the Same

Look at the first picture. Draw to make the pictures next to it look the same.

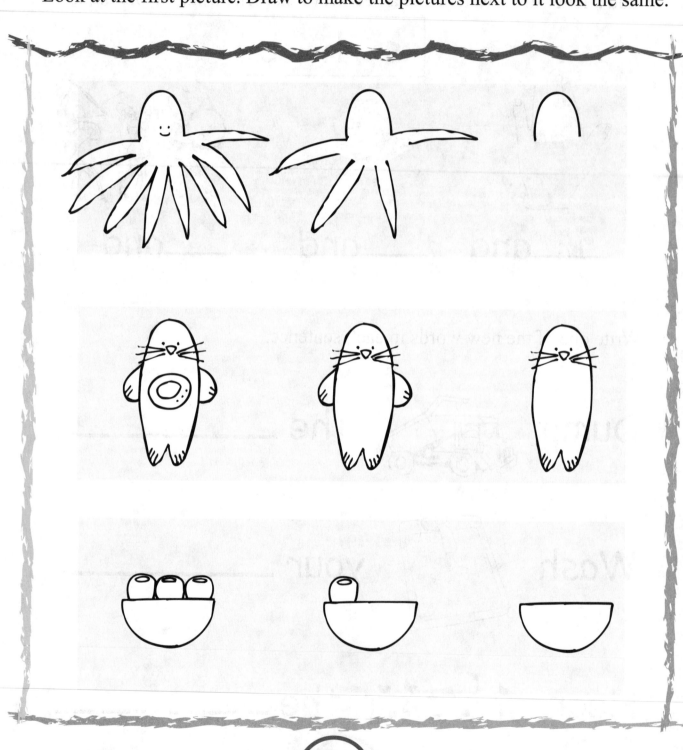

Rhyme Time

Circle the pictures that rhyme with frog.

Circle the pictures that rhyme with rock.

Circle the pictures that rhyme with top.

In a Puddle

The puppy's in a puddle.

The pig's in a puddle.

I'm in a puddle, too.

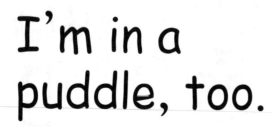

Pp

Sharpen Your Skills—Reading • EMC 9718 • © Evan-Moor Corp.

Listen for the Sound

Color the pictures that begin with the same sound as pig.

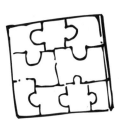

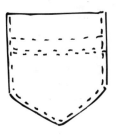

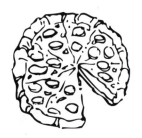

Pp

What Does It Say?

 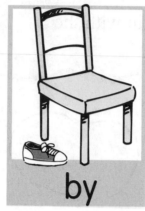 

on by under

Read the sentence. Circle the correct picture.

The is **on** the pot.

The  is **by** the pot.

The  is **under** the pot.

Pp

In the Pen

Draw: one pink pig

two black sheep

three yellow chicks

Puzzles, Puzzles, Puzzles

Put the puzzles together. Fill in ◯ yes or ◯ no.

Do you like pickles?

◯ yes   ◯ no

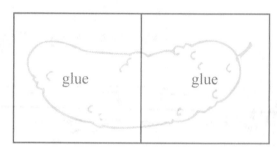

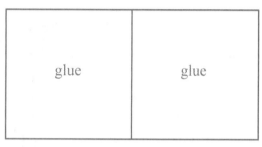

Do you like popcorn?

◯ yes   ◯ no

Do you like pancakes?

◯ yes   ◯ no

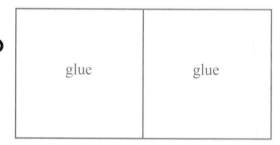

Do you like pizza?

◯ yes   ◯ no

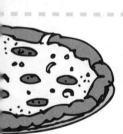

Be Quiet!

Quack, quack, quack.

Be quiet!

Quack, quack, quack.

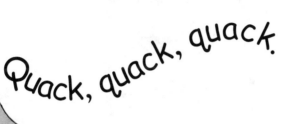

Be quiet!

Quack, quack, quack.

Quiet!

Qq

Listen for the Sound

Color the pictures that begin with the same sound as quack.

Quack

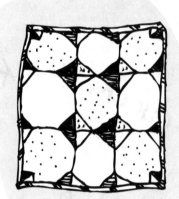

Qq

Sharpen Your Skills—Reading • EMC 9718 • © Evan-Moor Corp.

What Does It Say?

Match each word to a picture. Draw a line.

duck

frog

turtle

alligator

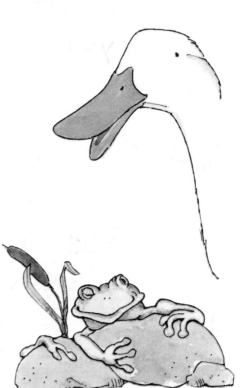

Yes or No?

Fill in ◯ yes or ◯ no.

1. A  says "Quack."

◯ yes ◯ no

2. An  says "Quack."

◯ yes ◯ no

3. A  says "Quack."

◯ yes ◯ no

4. A 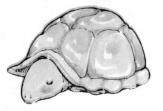 says "Quack."

◯ yes ◯ no

Qq

Seeing Words

Circle the words that are the same as the first word in each row.

jump	jump	run	jump
sleep	slip	sleep	sleep
quack	quack	quack	quiet
sit	sip	sit	sit
dog	dog	bog	dog
home	home	house	home

Qq

The Race

Run, rabbit, run.

Run, rooster, run.

Run, rhinoceros, run.

What a race!

Rr

Sharpen Your Skills—Reading • EMC 9718 • © Evan-Moor Corp.

Listen for the Sound

Cut and glue the pictures that begin with the same sound as rabbit.

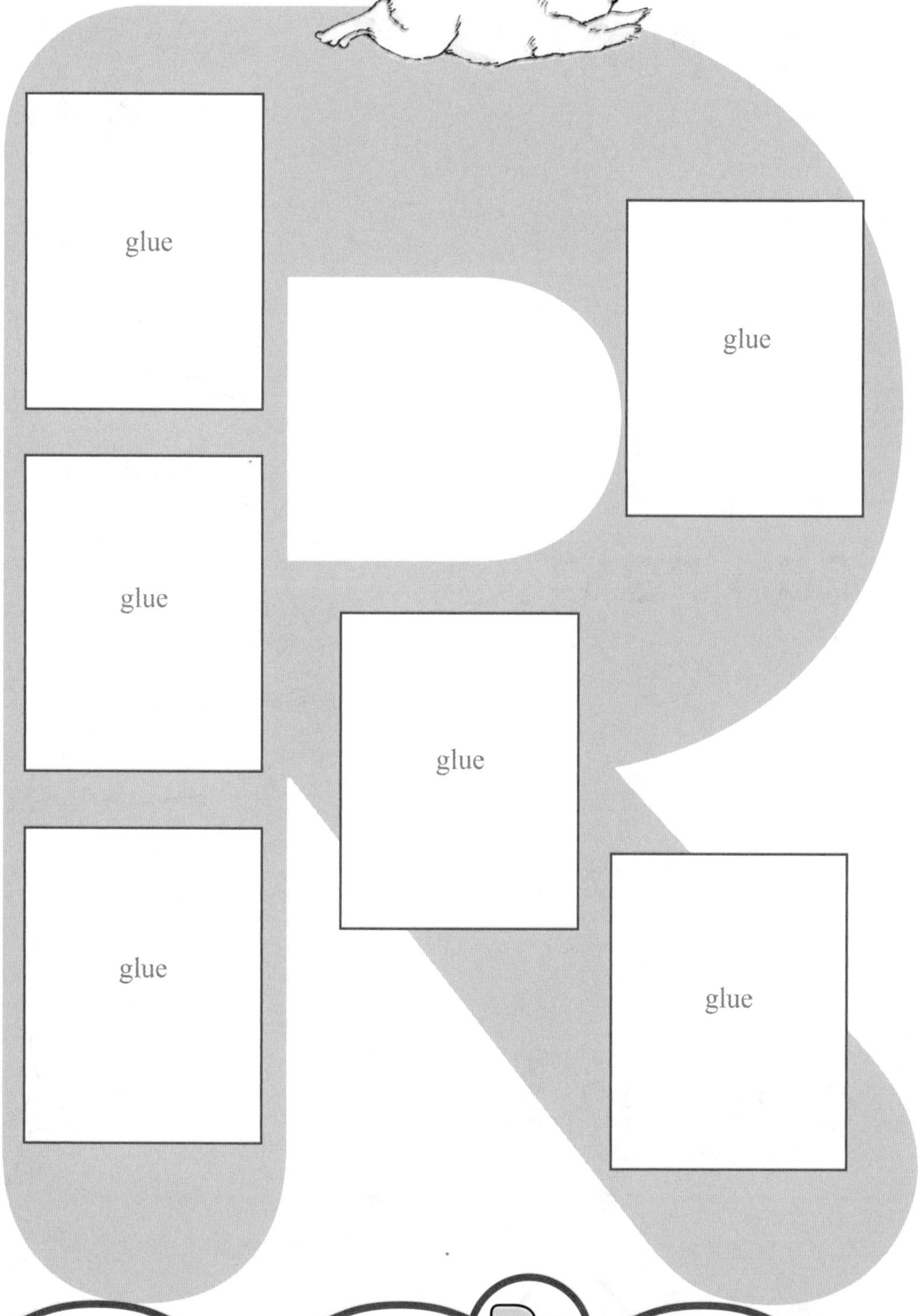

glue

glue

glue

glue

glue

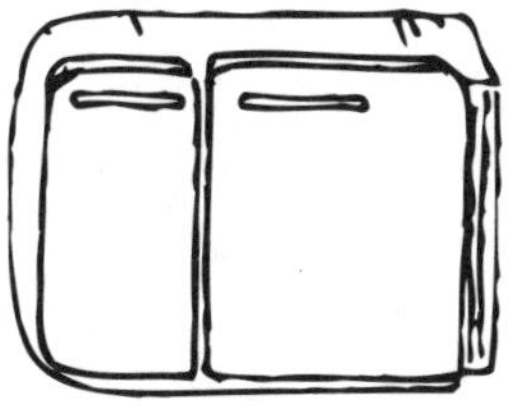

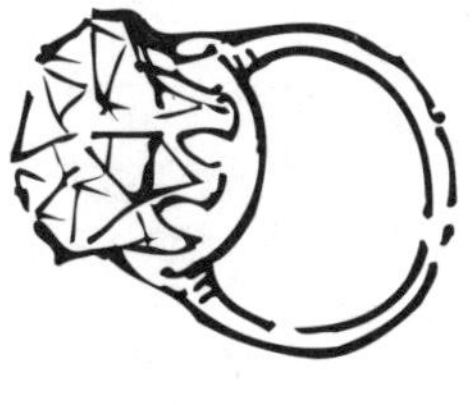

glue

Rr

What Does It Say?

Draw a line from each sentence to the correct picture.

I can run.

I can rest.

I can read.

Draw It!

Follow the pictures to draw a robot. Give the robot a name.

Rr

Find the Rhyme

Circle the pictures in each row that rhyme.

Rr

Sharpen Your Skills—Reading • EMC 9718 • © Evan-Moor Corp.

Sad Sam

See Sam.
Sam is sad.

See Sam.
Sam is so sad.
Sad, sad Sam.

 After You Read

Practice the story.
Make it sound sad.
Read it to an adult.

Listen for the Sound

6

Color the pictures that begin with the same sound as six.

Ss

What Does It Say?

Circle the word that tells about the picture. Write the word in the sentence.

sad   glad

Sam is _____.

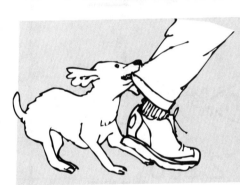

mad   sad

The dog is _____.

Bad   Dad

_____ kitty!

sad   glad

Sam is _____.

Ss

More Than One

Add **s** to the end of the word to mean more than one. Color the pictures.

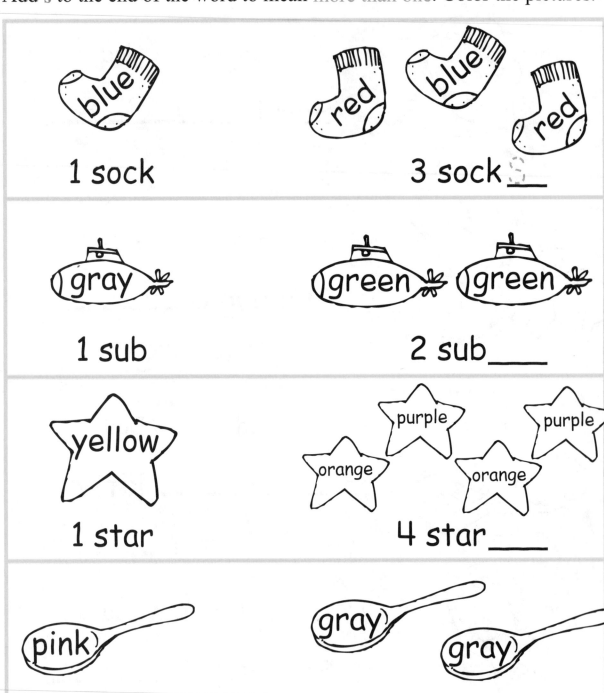

1 sock

3 sock___

1 sub

2 sub___

1 star

4 star___

1 spoon

2 spoon___

Ss

Dot-to-Dot

Connect the dots. Start with 1.

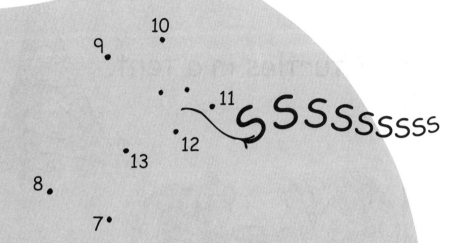

10
9
11
S S S S S S S S S S
12
13
8
7

14

4
6
3
5 15
1 18
2
20 17 16
19

What did you make?

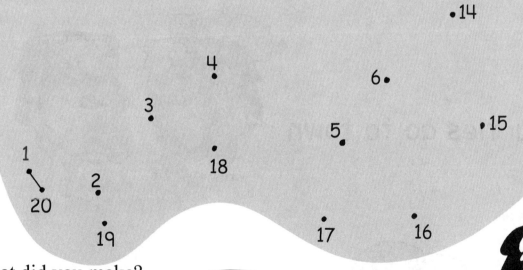

snail   snake   skunk

Ss

On the Trail

2 turtles in a tent.

2 turtles at the table.

2 turtles go to town.

2 tired turtles!

Tt

Listen for the Sound

Cut and glue the pictures that begin with the same sound as tent.

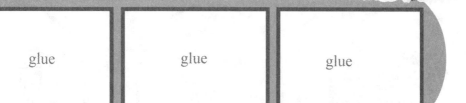

glue	glue	glue

glue

glue

glue

glue

glue

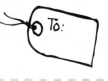

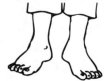

Tt

First or Last?

Say the name of each picture. Circle first or last to tell where you hear the **t** sound.

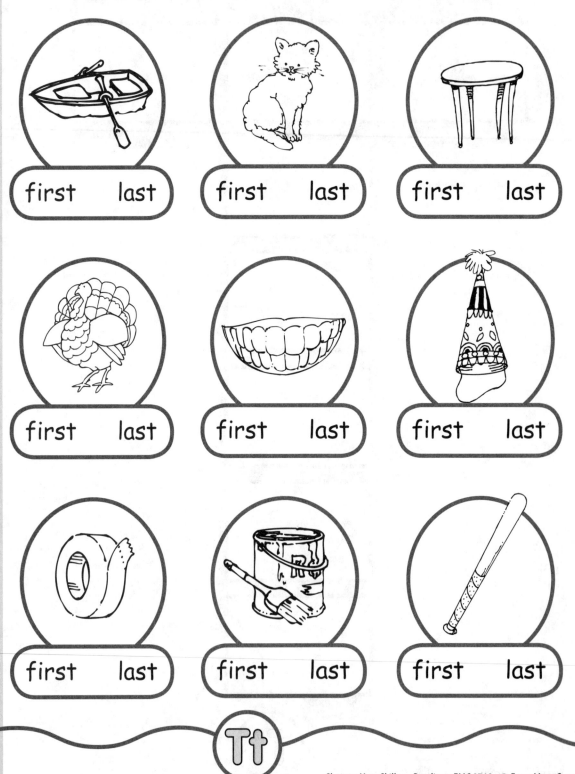

first	last
first	last
first	last
first	last
first	last
first	last
first	last
first	last
first	last

Skills: Blending Short Vowel Words

What Does It Say?

Look at each picture. Write the first letter and the last letter of each word.

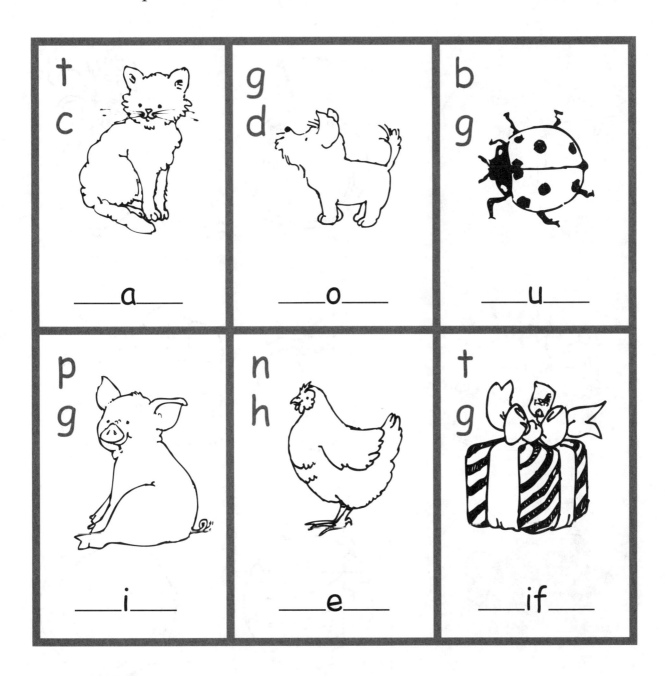

Circle the animals that have 4 legs.

What Will Come Next?

Circle the picture that shows what will happen next.

 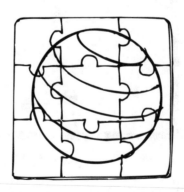 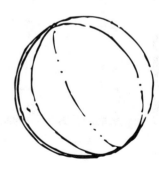

Sharpen Your Skills—Reading • EMC 9718 • © Evan-Moor Corp.

Up, up, up, up, up, up.

Down!

Uu

Listen for the Sound

Color the pictures that begin with the same sound as umbrella.

Sharpen Your Skills—Reading • EMC 9718 • © Evan-Moor Corp.

Up or Down?

Write up or down.

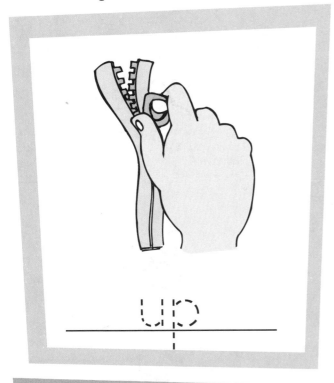

up

_____

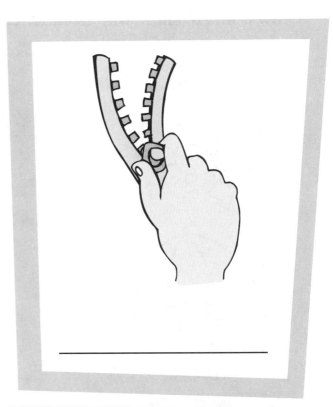

_____

_____

_____

Uu

Who Is Under the Umbrella?

Draw a line to show who is under each umbrella.

Uu

Read and Color

Read the words. Color the umbrella.

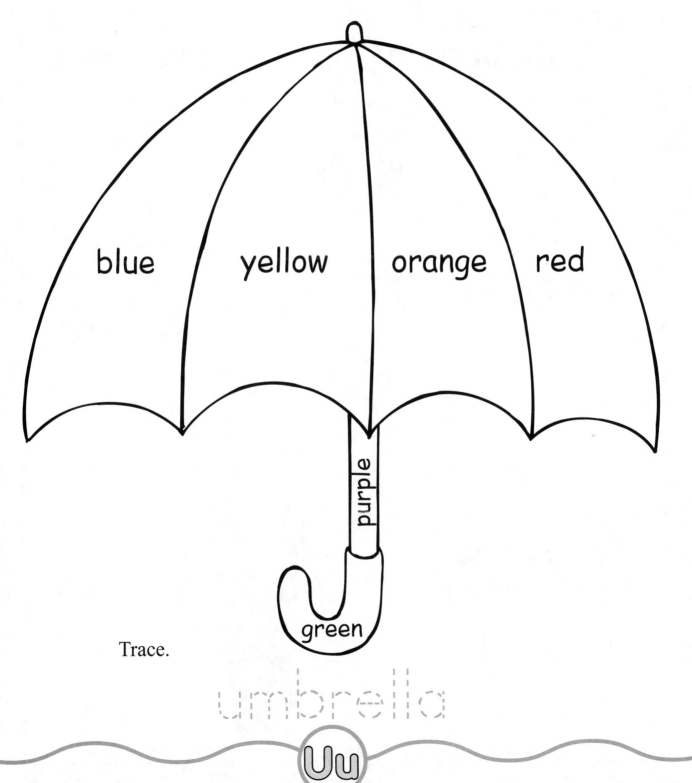

blue   yellow   orange   red

purple

green

Trace.

umbrella

Uu

Very Nice!

See my vest.
It's the best.

Very nice.

See my van.
It is tan.

Very nice.

See my vine.
It's just fine.

Very nice.

Vv

Listen for the Sound

Cut and glue the pictures that begin with the same sound as vine.

glue

glue

glue

glue

glue

glue

Vv

In the Garden

Color the vegetables.
Circle the vegetable you like the very best.

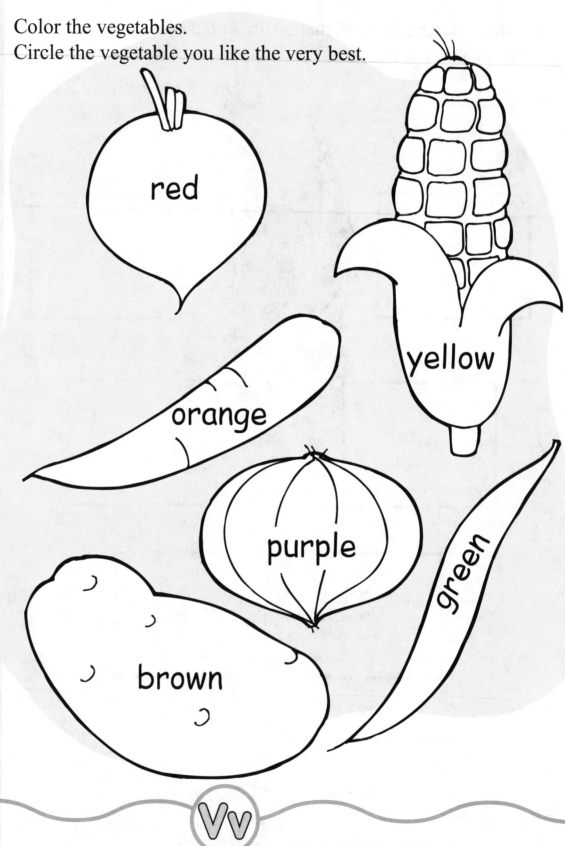

red

yellow

orange

purple

green

brown

Vv

What Does It Say?

Draw a line to match each word to a picture.

cave

vest

hive

stove

Draw It!

Follow the pictures to draw a van. Color the van.

Sharpen Your Skills—Reading • EMC 9718 • © Evan-Moor Corp.

Waffle Wagon

What's in the wagon?

weeds

What's in the wagon?

water

What's in the wagon?

wood

What's in the wagon?

Waffles!

Ww

Listen for the Sound

Color the pictures that begin with the same sound as wagon.

Waffle

Ww

What Does It Say?

Look at each picture.
Draw what you
should do.

Walk

Wait

Seeing Words

Circle the words in each row that are the same as the first word.

| **with** | with | will | with | with |

| **went** | won | went | went | went |

| **was** | was | was | saw | was |

| **what** | when | what | what | what |

| **wish** | wish | wish | wash | wish |

| **wag** | wag | wag | nag | wag |

Ww

Make a Wish

Follow the dots. Start with 1.

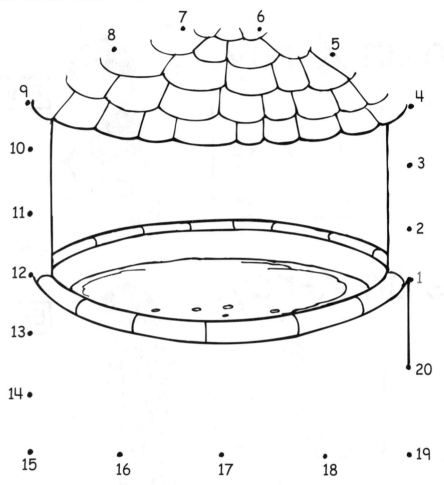

Have you made a wish at a wishing well?

○ yes   ○ no

What did you wish for?

_____

Fix It, Please!

Take an X-ray.

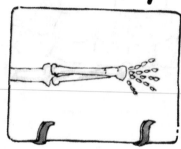  

Exit here.

Take an X-ray.

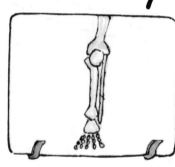  

Exit here.

Take an X-ray.

Exit here.

Xx

Sharpen Your Skills—Reading • EMC 9718 • © Evan-Moor Corp.

Listen for the Sound

Color the pictures that have the same ending sound as fox.
Write the end letter of each word.

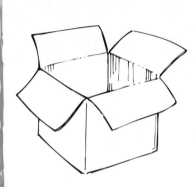

bo x___   a___   ca___

o___   si___   do___

What Does It Say?

Color the spaces with dots. Read the sign.

Follow the Directions

See the box.

Draw 3 balls in the box.

Color the balls blue.

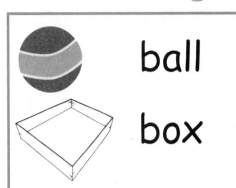

ball

box

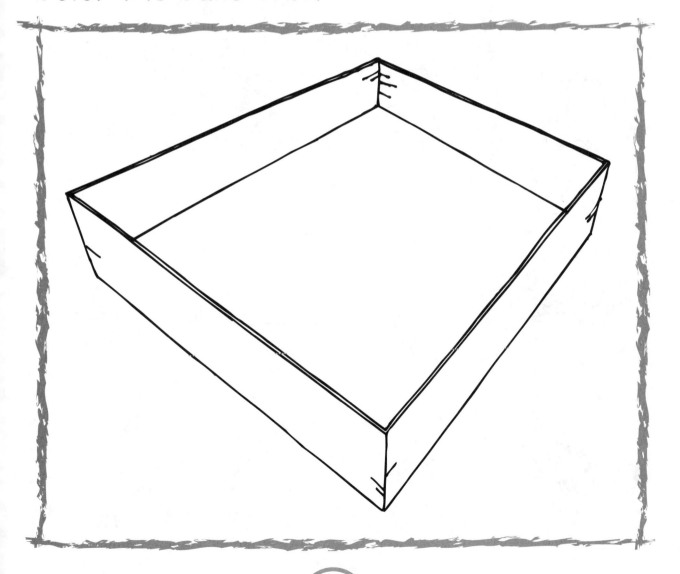

Rhyme Time

Circle the pictures that rhyme.

Time to Eat

Yum!

Yum!

Yuck!

Yy

Answer the Questions

Answer the questions. Write **yes** or **no**.

Do you like  ? _____

Do you like 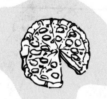 ? _____

Do you like  ? _____

Do you like  ? _____

Do you like  ? _____

Do you like  ? _____

Yy

Listen for the Sound

Cut and glue the pictures that begin with the same sound as yum.

yum

glue	glue

glue	glue

glue

| glue |

Yy

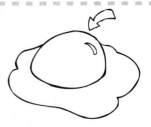

The -um Family

Write each word. Draw a line to the picture that matches.
Color the pictures.

g + um = _gum_

dr + um = _____

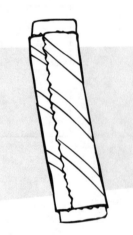

pl + um = _____

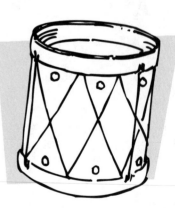

(Yy)

What Did Grandma Make?

Grandma made me a present. She made it out of yarn.
Color the shapes.

red = circles

blue = triangles

yellow = rectangles

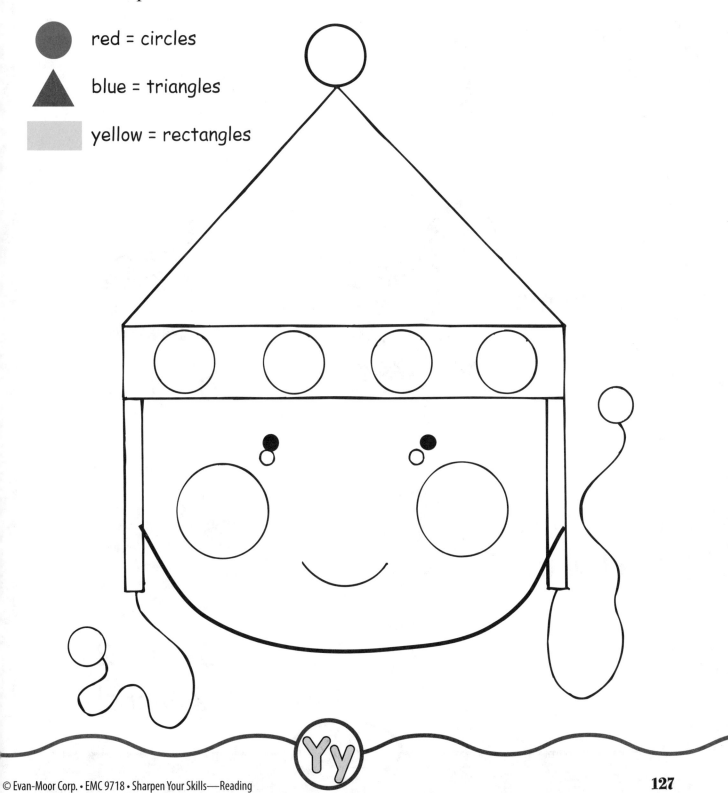

Beyond Zero

How many  ?

0   1   2

How many  ?

0   1   2

How many ?

0   1   2
Zillions!

Listen for the Sound

Color the pictures that begin with the same sound as zipper.

Zz

Seeing Words

Circle the words in each row that are the same as the first word.

zip	zap	zip	zip	zip

zonk	zonk	honk	zonk	zonk

zany	zany	sany	zany	zany

zing	zing	zing	sing	zing

zap	lap	zap	zap	zap

Zz

Tracking Form

Topic	Color in each page you complete.			
Unit 1 Letter A	4	5	6	7
Unit 2 Letter B	9	10	11	12
Unit 3 Letter C	14	15	16	17
Unit 4 Letter D	19	20	21	22
Unit 5 Letter E	24	25	26	27
Unit 6 Letter F	29	30	31	32
Unit 7 Letter G	34	35	36	37
Unit 8 Letter H	39	40	41	42
Unit 9 Letter I	44	45	46	47
Unit 10 Letter J	49	50	51	52
Unit 11 Letter K	54	55	56	57
Unit 12 Letter L	59	60	61	62
Unit 13 Letter M	64	65	66	67
Unit 14 Letter N	69	70	71	72
Unit 15 Letter O	74	75	76	77
Unit 16 Letter P	79	80	81	82
Unit 17 Letter Q	84	85	86	87
Unit 18 Letter R	89	90	91	92
Unit 19 Letter S	94	95	96	97
Unit 20 Letter T	99	100	101	102

Tracking Form

Topic		Color in each page you complete.			
Unit 21	Letter U	104	105	106	107
Unit 22	Letter V	109	110	111	112
Unit 23	Letter W	114	115	116	117
Unit 24	Letter X	119	120	121	122
Unit 25	Letter Y	124	125	126	127
Unit 26	Letter Z	129	130		

Sharpen Your Skills—Reading • EMC 9718 • © Evan-Moor Corp.

Answer Key

Page 4

Page 5

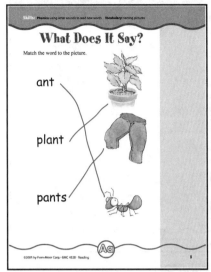

Page 6

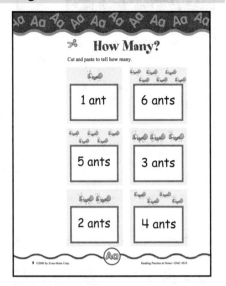

Page 7

Page 9

Page 10

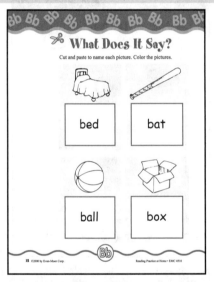

Page 11

Page 12

Page 14

Page 15

Listen for the Sound

Cut and paste the pictures that begin with the same sound as *car*.

Page 16

Color the Cat

Trace and write.

cat cat

Page 17

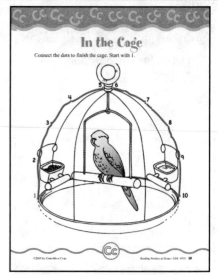

In the Cage

Connect the dots to finish the cage. Start with 1.

Page 19

Listen for the Sound

Color the pictures that begin with the same sound as *dog*.

donut

dog dish

door

duck

dinosaur

dime

Page 20

What Does It Say?

Draw a line to the right animal.

dog

cat

mouse

horse

frog

Page 21

Dudley Duck

Trace the – – – – lines. Color the picture.

Page 22

Skills: Using Prior Knowledge

A Good Place to Dig

Fill in ◯ yes or ◯ no.

This is a good place to dig.
● yes ◯ no

This is a good place to dig.
● yes ◯ no

This is a good place to dig.
◯ yes ● no

This is a good place to dig.
● yes ◯ no

Page 24

Listen for the Sound

Color the pictures that begin with the same sound as *egg*. Make an **X** on the pictures that begin with a different sound.

exit

elevator

escalator

envelope

elbow

elephant

Page 25

Seeing Words

Circle the words that are the same as the first word in each row.

egg	egg	eagle	egg
big	dig	big	big
little	little	little	lift
candy	dandy	candy	candy
good	good	dog	good

134

Sharpen Your Skills—Reading • EMC 9718 • © Evan-Moor Corp.

What Does It Say?

Circle the word that names the picture.

	(ball)	rug
	pen	(cat)
	(egg)	leg
	book	(ant)
	(dog)	moon
	sun	(cap)

Is It Real?

Fill in ○ yes or ○ no.

Is it real? ○ yes ● no
Is it real? ● yes ○ no
Is it real? ● yes ○ no
Is it real? ● yes ○ no

Listen for the Sound

Cut and paste to show which pictures begin with the same sound as fish.

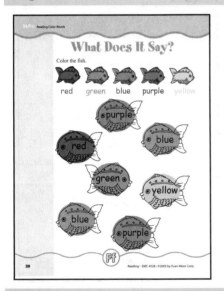

What Does It Say?

Color the fish.

red   green   blue   purple   yellow

Rhyme Time

Circle the pictures in each line that rhyme.

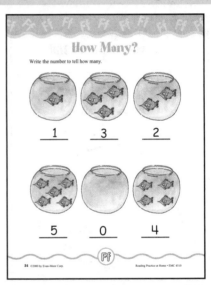

How Many?

Write the number to tell how many.

1   3   2

5   0   4

Listen for the Sound

Color the pictures that begin with the sound that g makes in goat.

gift   gum   gorilla   golf club   gate   girl   guitar

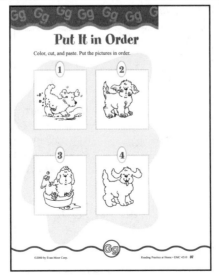

Put It in Order

Color, cut, and paste. Put the pictures in order.

1   2   3   4

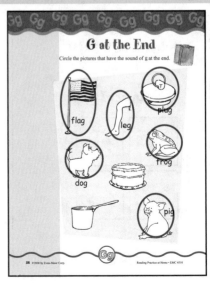

G at the End

Circle the pictures that have the sound of g at the end.

flag   leg   plug   frog   dog   pig

Page 37

What Do You Think?

Trace.

good   bad

Write good or bad.

bad   good

Page 39

Listen for the Sound

Circle the pictures that begin with the same sound as hippo.

hat   horse
house
hot dog   hen
helicopter   heart

Page 40

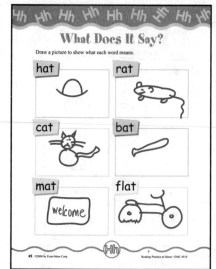

What Does It Say?

Draw a picture to show what each word means.

hat   rat
cat   bat
mat   flat

Page 41

The House on the Hill

Follow the dots to make a hill.
Color the hill.
Draw a house on top.

Page 42

Is He Happy?

Fill in ○ yes or ○ no.

Is he happy? ○ yes ● no

Is he happy? ● yes ○ no

Is he happy? ○ yes ● no

Is he happy? ● yes ○ no

Page 44

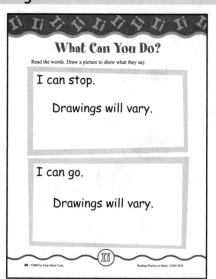

What Can You Do?

Read the words. Draw a picture to show what they say.

I can stop.

Drawings will vary.

I can go.

Drawings will vary.

Page 45

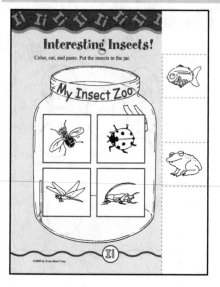

Interesting Insects!

Color, cut, and paste. Put the insects in the jar.

My Insect Zoo

Page 46

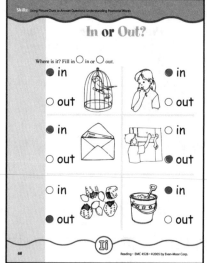

In or Out?

Where is it? Fill in ○ in or ○ out.

● in ○ out   ● in ○ out
● in ○ out   ○ in ● out
○ in ● out   ● in ○ out

Page 47

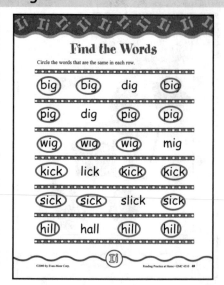

Find the Words

Circle the words that are the same in each row.

big   big   dig   big
pig   dig   pig   pig
wig   wig   wig   mig
kick   lick   kick   kick
sick   sick   slick   sick
hill   hall   hill   hill

Page 49

Skills: Listening for the /j/ Sound; Using Scissors

Listen for the Sound

Cut and glue the pictures that begin with the same sound as jar.

©2005 by Evan-Moor Corp. • EMC 4528 • Reading   49

Page 50

What Does It Say?

Match the word to the picture. Color the pictures.

jar

jam

jet

jeep

52 ©2000 by Evan-Moor Corp.   Reading Practice at Home • EMC 4510

Page 51

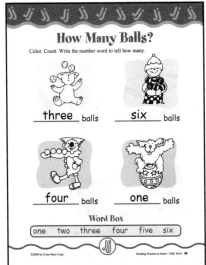

How Many Balls?

Color. Count. Write the number word to tell how many.

three balls   six balls

four balls   one balls

Word Box

one	two	three	four	five	six

©2000 by Evan-Moor Corp.   Reading Practice at Home • EMC 4510   53

Page 52

Just Jack

Color all the pieces of the puzzle that have a dot.

See Jack.

54 ©2000 by Evan-Moor Corp.   Reading Practice at Home • EMC 4510

Page 54

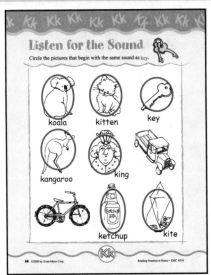

Listen for the Sound

Circle the pictures that begin with the same sound as key.

koala   kitten   key

kangaroo   king

ketchup   kite

56 ©2000 by Evan-Moor Corp.   Reading Practice at Home • EMC 4510

Page 55

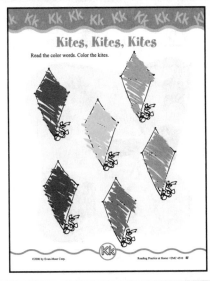

Kites, Kites, Kites

Read the color words. Color the kites.

©2000 by Evan-Moor Corp.   Reading Practice at Home • EMC 4510   57

Page 56

Skills: Using Prior Knowledge; Distinguishing Real and Make-Believe

Kindergarten

Could it happen in kindergarten? Fill in ◯ yes or ◯ no.

◯ yes ◯ no   ◯ yes ◯ no

◯ yes ◯ no   ◯ yes ◯ no

56 ©2005 by Evan-Moor Corp. • Reading

Page 57

New Words

The pictures show what each new k word means. Draw a line to show who would use each thing.

kennel

kerchief

kettle

kayak

©2000 by Evan-Moor Corp.   Reading Practice at Home • EMC 4510   59

Page 59

Skills: Listening for the /l/ Sound at the Beginning and Ending of Words

Listen for the Sound

Say the name of each picture. Do you hear the l sound first or last?
Fill in ◯ first or ◯ last.

●first ◯last   ◯first ●last   ●first ◯last

●first ◯last   ◯first ●last   ●first ◯last

●first ◯last   ◯first ●last   ◯first ●last

©2005 by Evan-Moor Corp. • EMC 4528 • Reading   59

Page 60

Little or Large?
Color the pictures. Put an X on the little one.

Page 61

Look! I can make new words!

Start with look.	l o o k
Take off the l. Put on a b.	b o o k
Take off the b. Put on an h.	h o o k
Take off the h. Put on a c.	c o o k
Take off the c. Put on br.	b r o o k

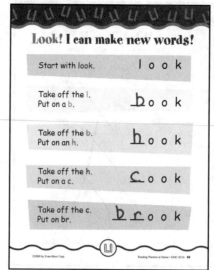

Page 62

What's for Lunch?
Color the food.

Page 64

Listen for the Sound
Color the pictures that begin with the same sound as mouse.

mail   mitten   moose   mouse   mitt   monkey   map

Page 65

Match the Mittens
Cut and paste to make pairs.

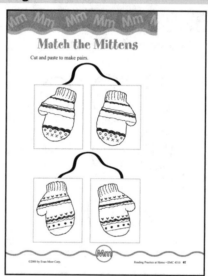

Page 66

Skills: Recalling Story Details

Where Am I?
Draw a line to make a match.

Find my house.
Find my tepee.
Find my hole.

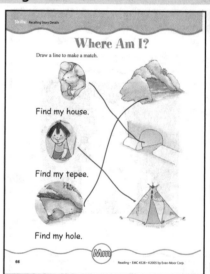

Page 67

In the Night Sky
Connect the dots. Start with 1. Color the picture.

Have you ever seen the moon?   Answers will vary.
yes   no

Page 69

Listen for the Sound
Cut and paste to show what pictures begin with the same sound as net.

Page 70

No, No, No
Write No or Yes.

The ball is red. No
The ball is green. No
The ball is yellow. No
The ball is brown. No

Do you have a ball? Answers will vary.
Do you play with a ball? _____

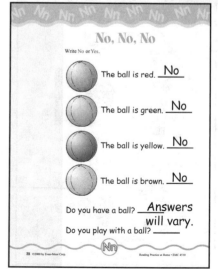

Page 71

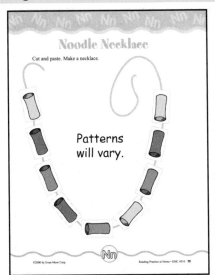

Noodle Necklace

Cut and paste. Make a necklace.

Patterns will vary.

Page 72

Naughty or Nice?

Circle the word to tell whether they are naughty or nice.

- ● naughty ○ nice
- ○ naughty ● nice
- ○ naughty ● nice
- ● naughty ○ nice

Page 74

Listen for the Sound

Color the pictures that begin like otter.

otter, ostrich, olive, octopus

Page 75

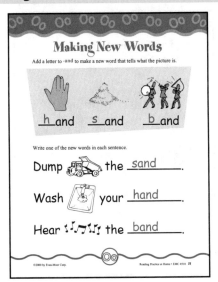

Making New Words

Add a letter to -and to make a new word that tells what the picture is.

h and   s and   b and

Write one of the new words in each sentence.

Dump the ___sand___.

Wash your ___hand___.

Hear the ___band___.

Page 76

Make Them Look the Same

Look at the first thing. Make the others the same.

Page 77

Rhyme Time

Color the pictures that rhyme with frog.

dog, log

Color the pictures that rhyme with rock.

lock, sock

Color the pictures that rhyme with top.

mop, drop, stop

Page 79

Listen for the Sound

Color the pictures to show the words that begin with the sound that p stands for.

pocket, potato, pencil, puzzle, popcorn, penny, pizza, pumpkin, pig, paint

Page 80

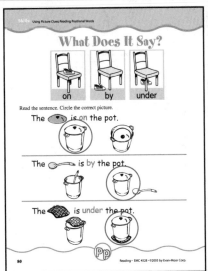

What Does It Say?

on   by   under

Read the sentence. Circle the correct picture.

The ___ is on the pot.

The ___ is by the pot.

The ___ is under the pot.

Page 81

In the Pen

Draw: one pink pig
three black sheep
three yellow chicks

Drawings will vary.
There should be
1 pig, 2 sheep, and
3 chicks.

Page 82

Puzzles, Puzzles, Puzzles

Put the puzzles together. Answer yes or no.

Do you like pickles?

(yes) (no)

Answers will vary.

Do you like popcorn?

(yes) (no)

Answers will vary.

Do you like pancakes?

(yes) (no)

Answers will vary.

Do you like pizza?

Answers will vary.

(yes) (no)

Page 83

Listen for the Sound

Color the pictures that have the same beginning sound as quack.

Quack

queen

quarter

quilt

quail

question mark

Page 85

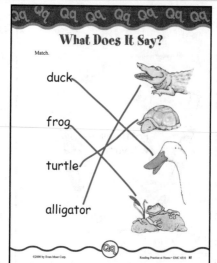

What Does It Say?

Match.

duck

frog

turtle

alligator

Page 86

Skills: Reading Story Details

Yes or No?

Fill in ◯ yes or ◯ no.

1. A _____ says "Quack."
   ◯ yes ● no

2. An _____ says "Quack."
   ◯ yes ● no

3. A _____ says "Quack."
   ● yes ◯ no

4. A _____ says "Quack."
   ◯ yes ● no

Page 87

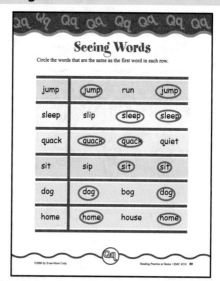

Seeing Words

Circle the words that are the same as the first word in each row.

jump	(jump)	run	(jump)
sleep	slip	(sleep)	(sleep)
quack	(quack)	(quack)	quiet
sit	sip	(sit)	(sit)
dog	(dog)	bog	(dog)
home	(home)	house	(home)

Page 89

Listen for the Sound

Cut and paste to show which pictures begin with the same sound as rabbit.

Page 90

What Does It Say?

Draw a line from the sentence to the correct picture.

I can run.

I can rest!

I can read.

Page 91

Draw It!

Draw and color. Give the robot a name.

Drawings and names will vary.

Page 92

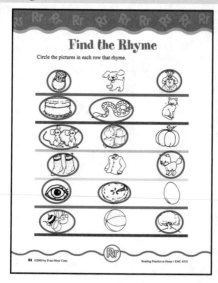

Find the Rhyme

Circle the pictures in each row that rhyme.

Page 94

Listen for the Sound 6

Color the pictures that begin with the same sound as *six*.

sock — sun — sandwich

ladder — saddle — seal

sandal — bee — scissors

Page 95

What Does It Say?

Circle the word that tells about the picture. Write the word in the sentence.

(sad) glad
Sam is **sad**.

(mad) sad
The dog is **mad**.

(Bad) Dad
Bad kitty!

sad (glad)
Sam is **glad**.

Page 96

More Than One

Add *s* to the end of the word to mean more than one. Color the pictures.

1 sock	3 sock **S**
1 sub	2 sub **S**
1 star	4 star **S**
1 spoon	2 spoon **S**

Page 97

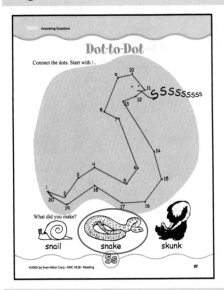

Dot-to-Dot

Connect the dots. Start with 1.

SSSSssss

What did you make?

snail — snake — skunk

Page 99

Listen for the Sound

Cut and paste the pictures that begin with the same sound as *tent*.

Page 100

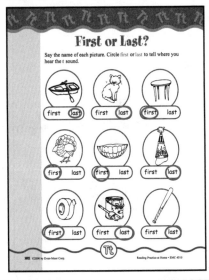

First or Last?

Say the name of each picture. Circle *first* or *last* to tell where you hear the *t* sound.

first last — first last — first last

first last — first last — first last

first last — first last — first last

Page 101

What Does It Say?

Look at each picture. Write the first letter and the last letter of each word.

| c a t | d o g | b u g |
| p i g | h e n | g i f t |

Circle the animals that have 4 legs.

Page 102

What Will Come Next?

Circle the picture that shows what will happen next.

Page 104

Listen for the Sound

Color the pictures that begin with the same sound as *umbrella*.

umbrella

up

umpire

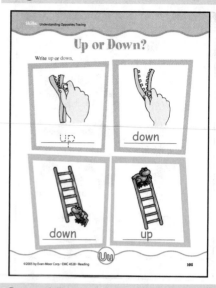

Up or Down?

Write up or down.

up   down

down   up

Who Is Under the Umbrella?

Draw a line to show who is under the umbrella.

Read and Color

Read the words. Color the umbrella.

Trace.

umbrella

Listen for the Sound

Cut and paste to show which pictures begin with the same sound as vine.

In the Garden

Color the vegetables.
Circle the one you like the very best.

Answers will vary.

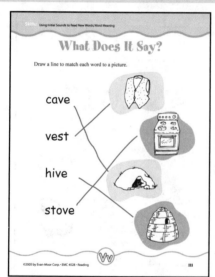

What Does It Say?

Draw a line to match each word to a picture.

cave

vest

hive

stove

Listen for the Sound

Color the pictures that begin with the same sound as wagon.

Waffles!

wall
web
window   watch   windmill
worm   walrus

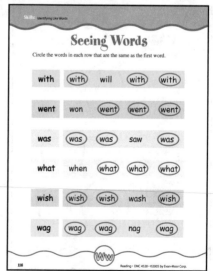

Seeing Words

Circle the words in each row that are the same as the first word.

with	with	will	with	with
went	won	went	went	went
was	was	was	saw	was
what	when	what	what	what
wish	wish	wish	wash	wish
wag	wag	wag	nag	wag

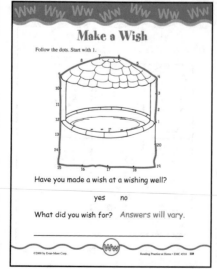

Make a Wish

Follow the dots. Start with 1.

Have you made a wish at a wishing well?

yes   no

What did you wish for?   Answers will vary.

_____

Page 119

Page 120

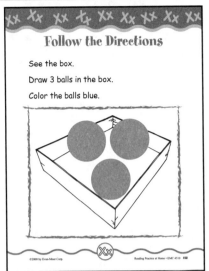

Page 121

Page 122

Page 125

Page 126

Page 127

Page 129

Page 130

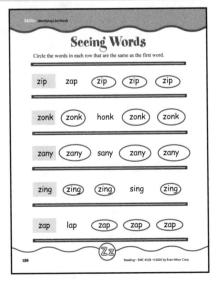

Contents

Skills:

Writing Numbers

Counting

Practice writing your numbers.

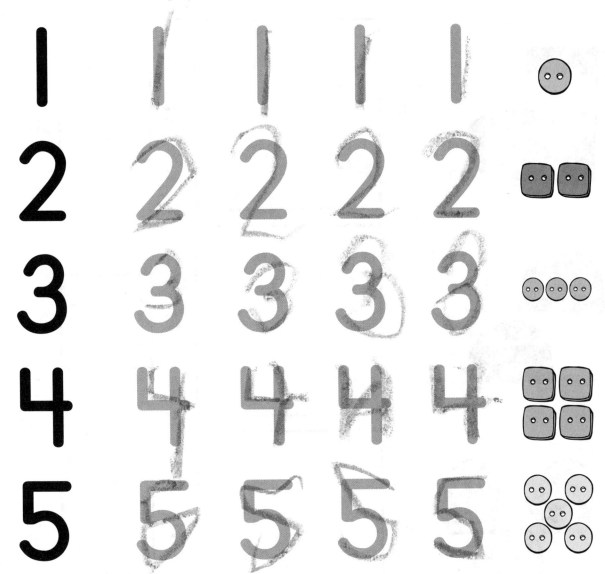

Count the buttons. Write the correct number.

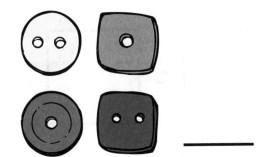

_____

_____

Things I wear

Adding 1

Skills:

Adding One More

Things I Wear

Draw one more. Count how many. Write the number.

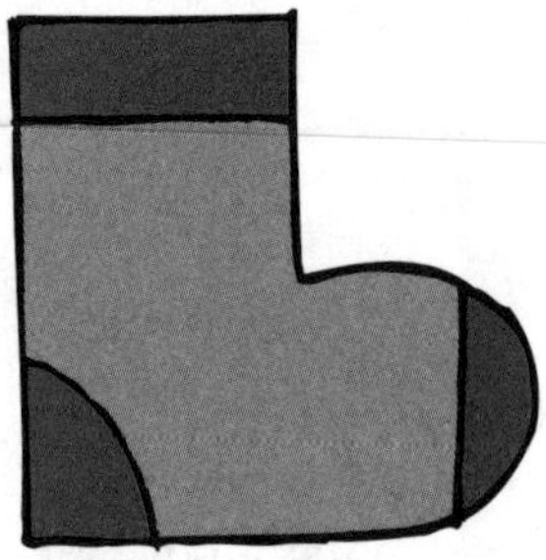

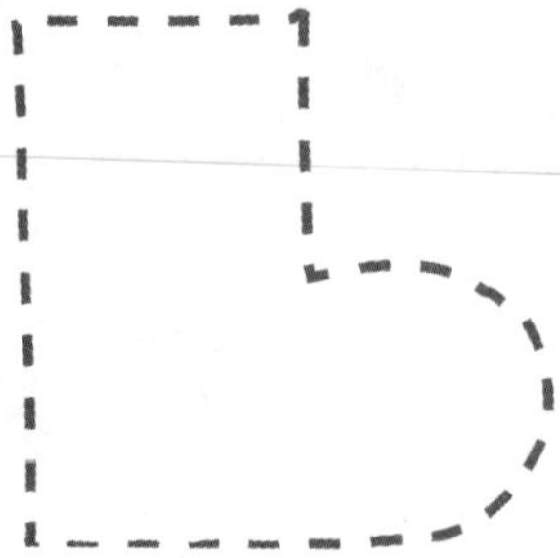

 + = 2

 + =

 + =

 + =

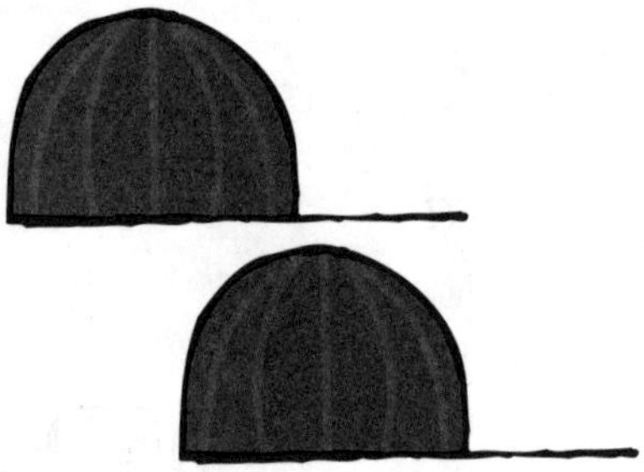

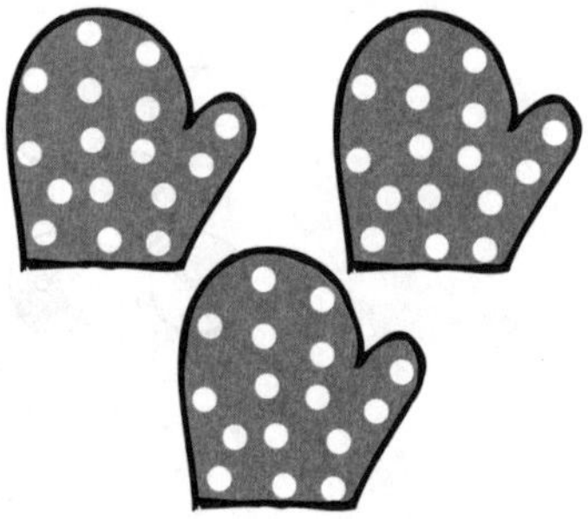

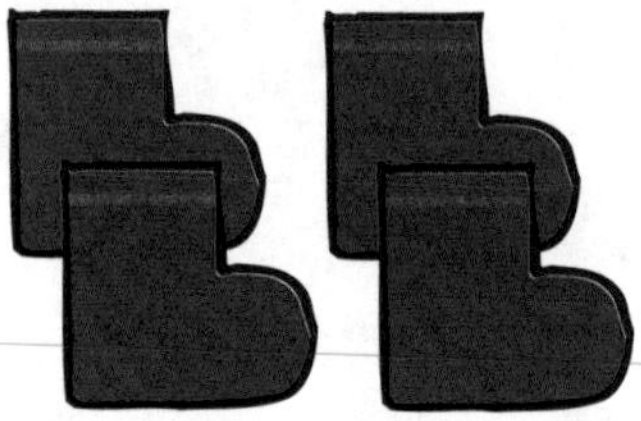

Color the bigger one.

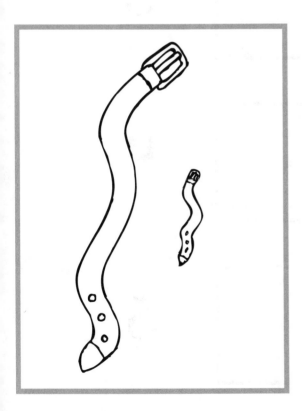

Things I wear

Put Them in Order

Skills: Number Order

Cut and paste. Count the buttons.

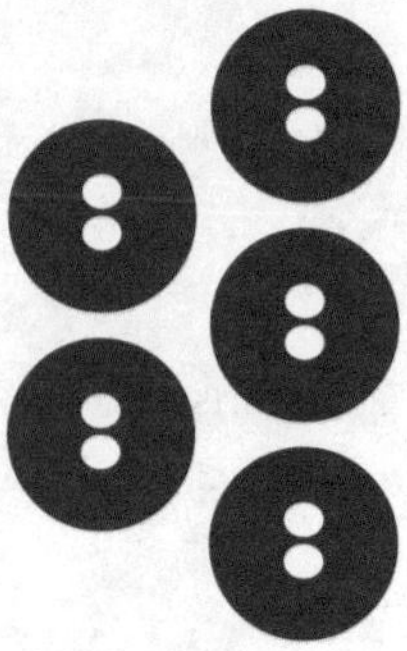

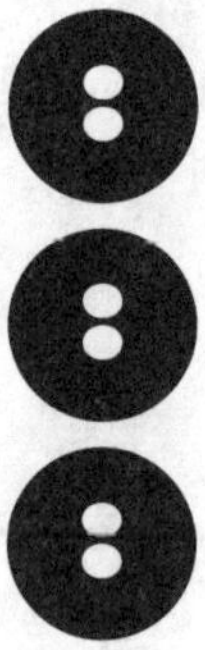

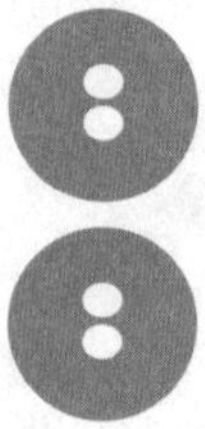

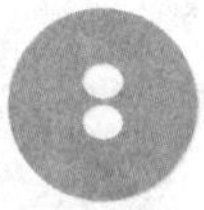

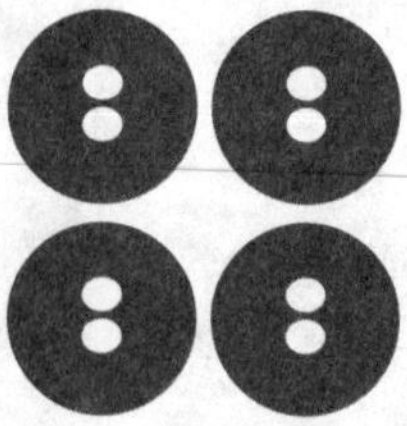

one	paste	1
two	paste	2
three	paste	3
four	paste	4
five	paste	5

Skills:
One-to-One
Correspondence

Color the hats. Draw a line from a to a .

Things I wear

Which has more?

Mitten, Mitten

Color the mittens. Follow the pattern.

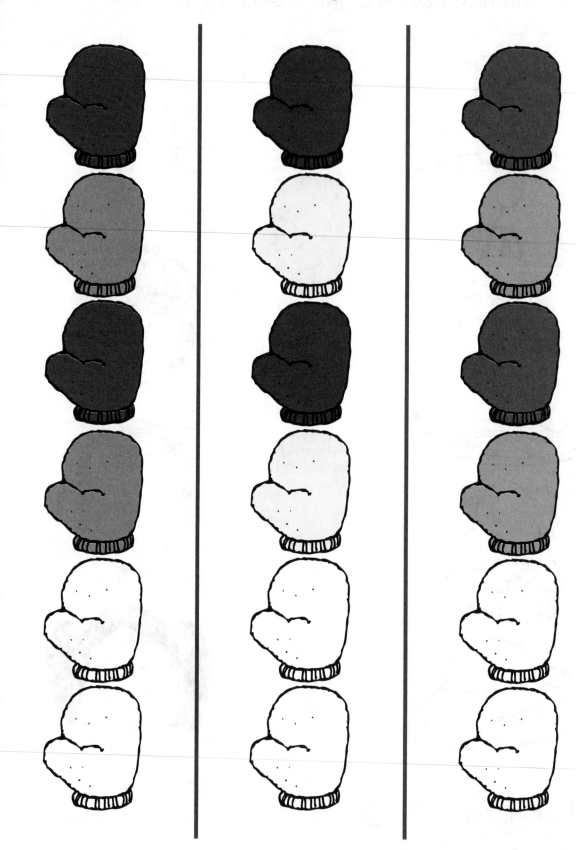

Skills:

One-to-One
Correspondence

Counting

Draw a 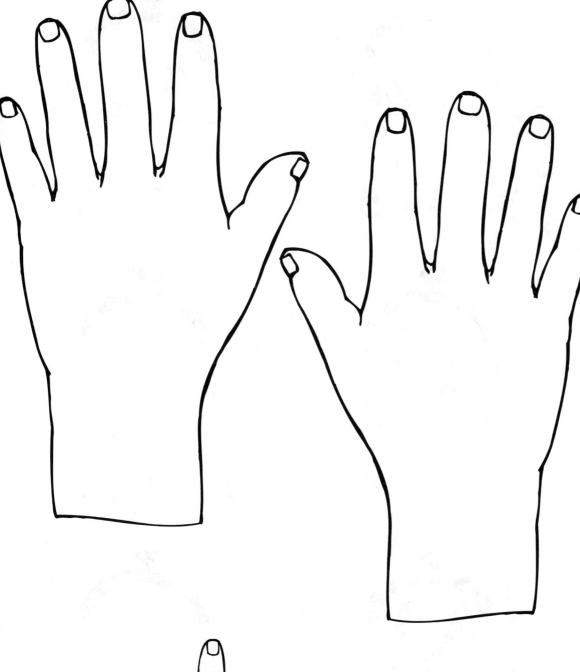 on each finger.

How many ⋀s? _____

How many ◯s? _____

Things I wear

Pennies in My Purse

Count the pennies in each purse. Circle the number.

3   4   5

1   2   3

2   3   4

1   2   3

3   4   5

0   1   2

Things I Wear

Sharpen Your Skills—Math • EMC 9718 • © Evan-Moor Corp.

Skills:

Number Order

Connect the dots. Start with 1.

4

•5

3•

2•

1•   •6

Will 🐰 stay dry?   yes   no

Things I wear

Graph a Jacket

Skills:

Counting

Graphing

Look at the jacket.

Color one square for each.

Skills:

Writing Numbers

Counting

Write the numbers.

How many shoes?

How many socks?

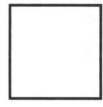

How many shirts?

How many coats?

How many hats?

Things I wear

Count the dots. Write the number to tell how many.

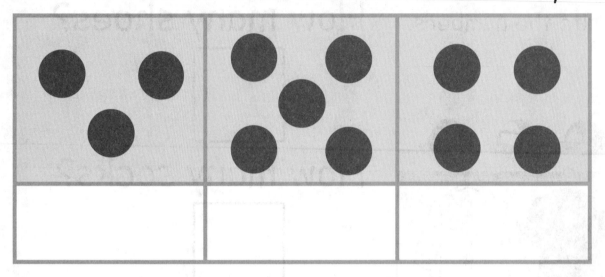

Continue the pattern.

Count the pennies. Fill in the circle next to the correct number.

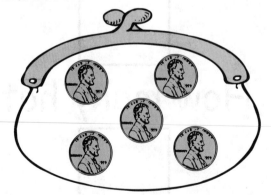

○ 3

○ 4

○ 5

Count the bugs. Circle the number to tell how many.

Skills:

Understanding Numbers

1 2 3 4 5   1 2 3 4 5   1 2 3 4 5

1 2 3 4 5   1 2 3 4 5   1 2 3 4 5

0 1 2 3 4 5   0 1 2 3 4 5   0 1 2 3 4 5

creepy crawlies

Skills:

Size
Comparisons

Counting

Creepy Crawlies

Circle the big bugs.

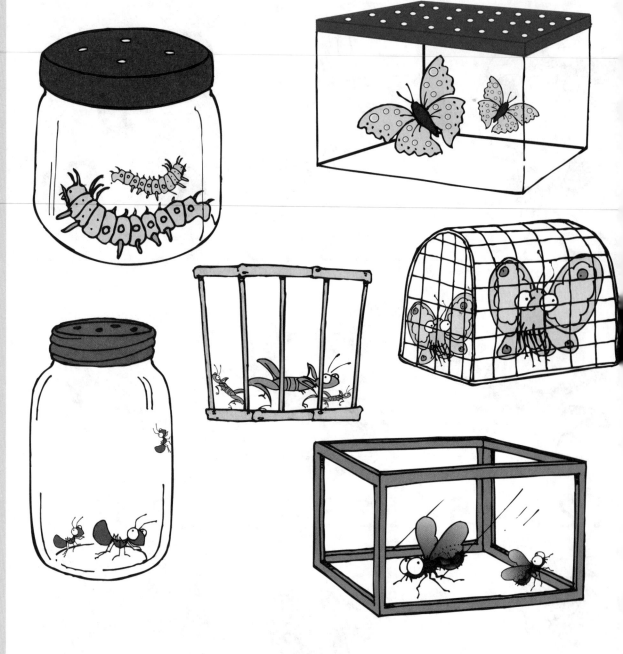

How many big bugs are there? _____

How many little bugs are there? _____

How many bugs are there in all? _____

Skills:
Addition
Number Words

Tom put in one bug.
Draw it.
Juan put in two bugs.
Draw them.

Maria put in two bugs.
Draw them.
Sue put in three bugs.
Draw them.

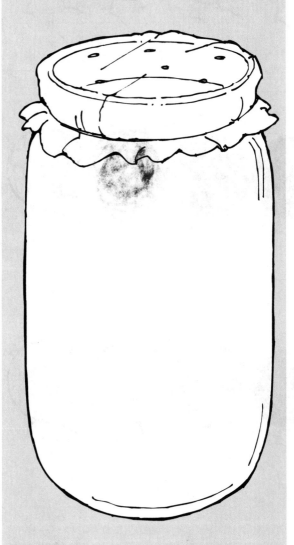

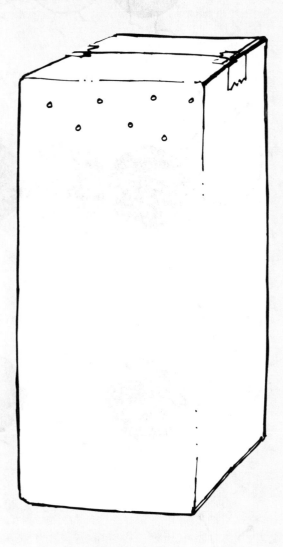

How many bugs
are in the jar? _____

How many bugs
are in the box? _____

creepy crawlies

So Many Colors!

Color to finish the patterns.

Cut and paste. Put the bugs under the correct number.

Three

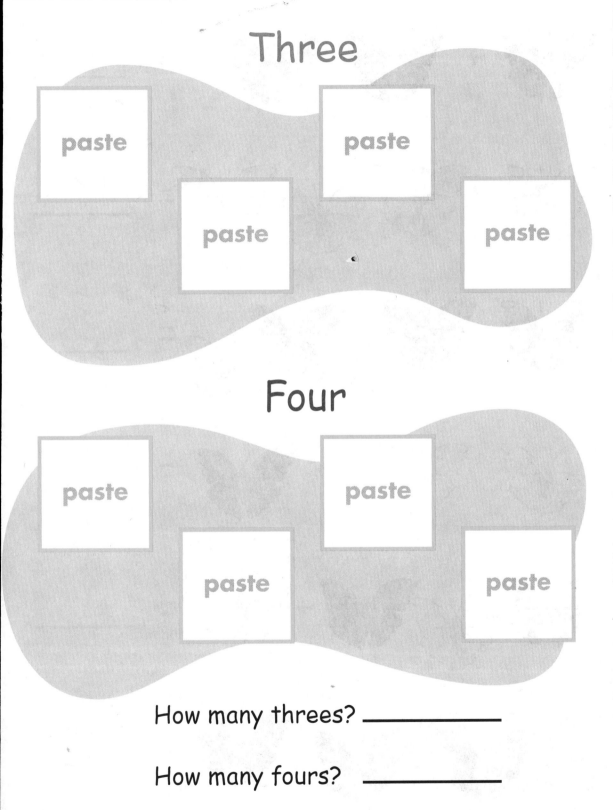

Four

How many threes? _____

How many fours? _____

Beautiful Butterflies

Write the number.

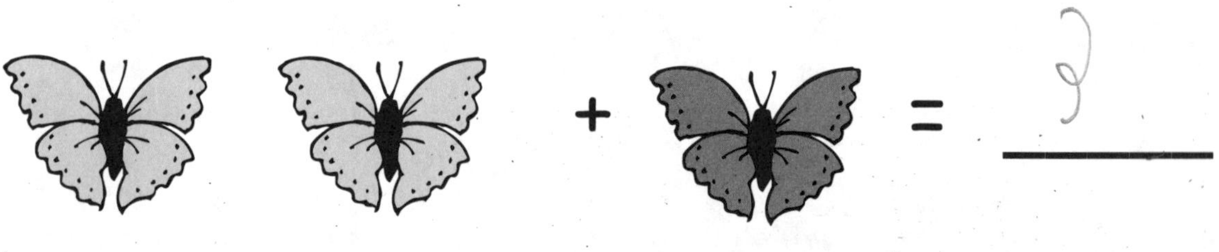

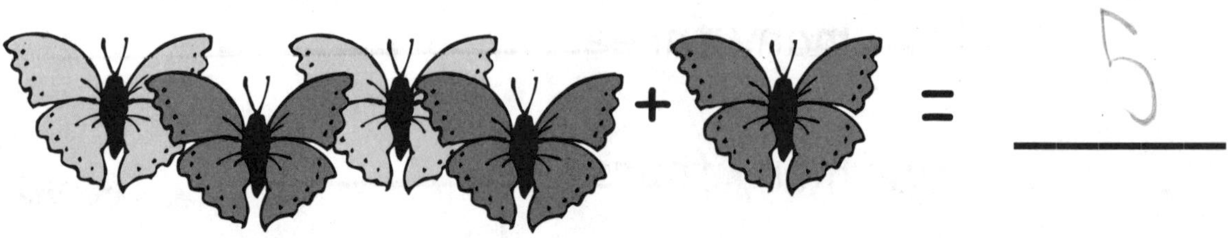

🦋 + 🦋 🦋 = 3

🦋 + 🦋 🦋 🦋 = 4

🦋 + 🦋 🦋 🦋 🦋 = 5

🦋 🦋 + 🦋 = 2

🦋 🦋 🦋 + 🦋 = 4

🦋 🦋 🦋 🦋 + 🦋 = 5

Skills:

Counting

Graphing

Count the creatures.

Color spaces on the graph to tell how many.

Which had the most? _____

Creepy Crawlies

Squirmy Worms

Write the number.

🐛 - 🐛 = _____

🐛🐛 - 🐛 = _____

🐛🐛 - 🐛 = _____

🐛🐛 - 🐛 = _____

🐛🐛 - 🐛 = _____

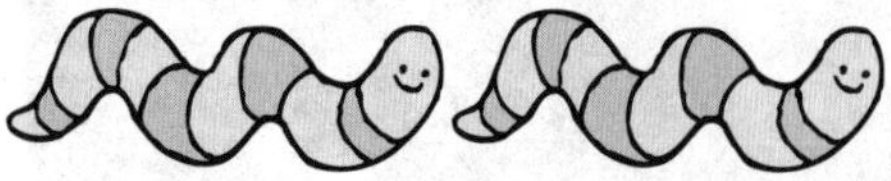

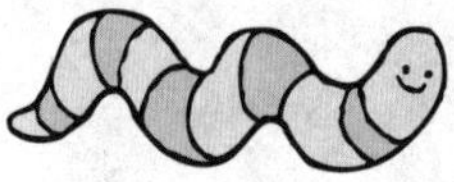

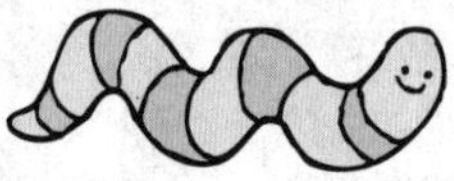

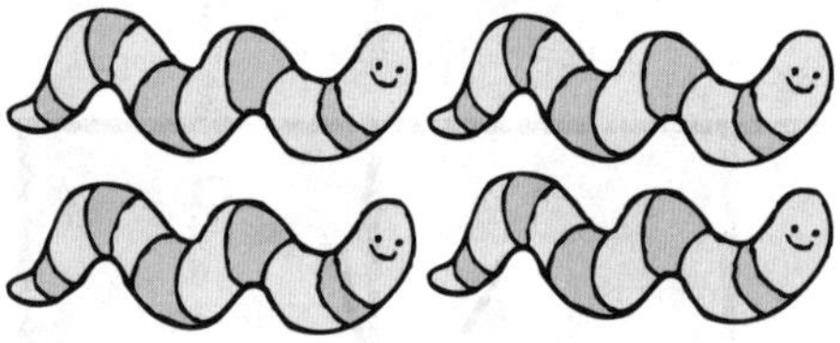

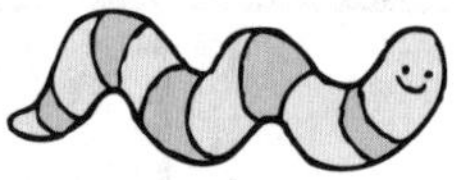

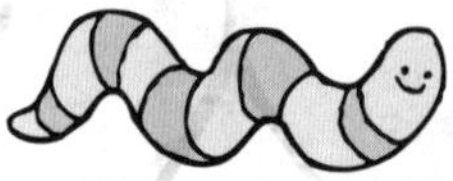

🐛🐛 - 0 = _____

Sharpen Your Skills—Math • EMC 9718 • © Evan-Moor Corp.

Creepy Crawlies

Write the number.

Skills:

Addition

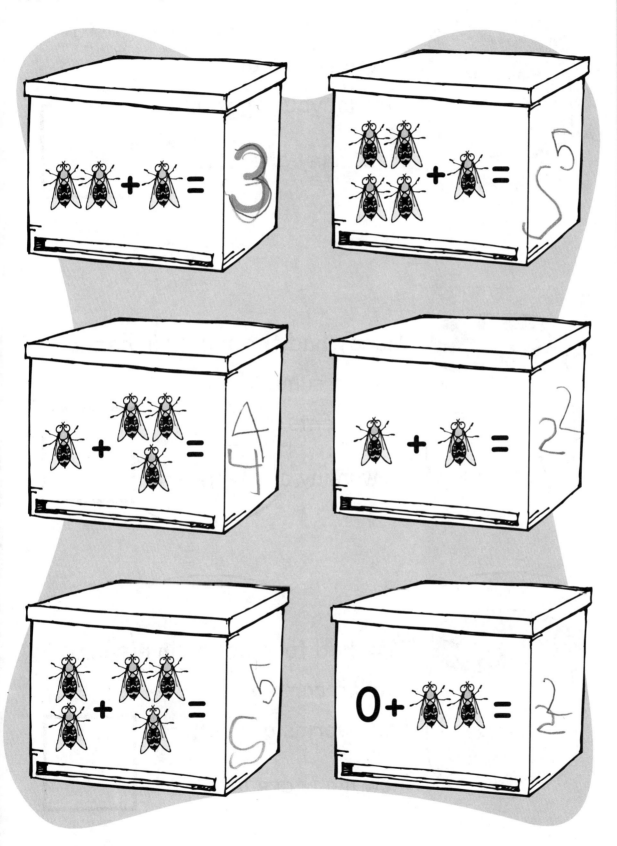

creepy crawlies

They Got Away

Creepy Crawlies

Matt had five ladybugs in his jar.

The lid came off.

Five ladybugs got out.

How many are left?

Mandy had three ants in her jar.

The lid came off.

Three ants got out.

How many are left?

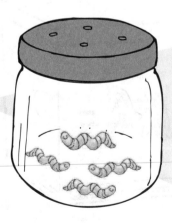

Max had four worms in his jar.

The lid came off.

Four worms got out.

How many are left?

Fill in the circle under the correct number.

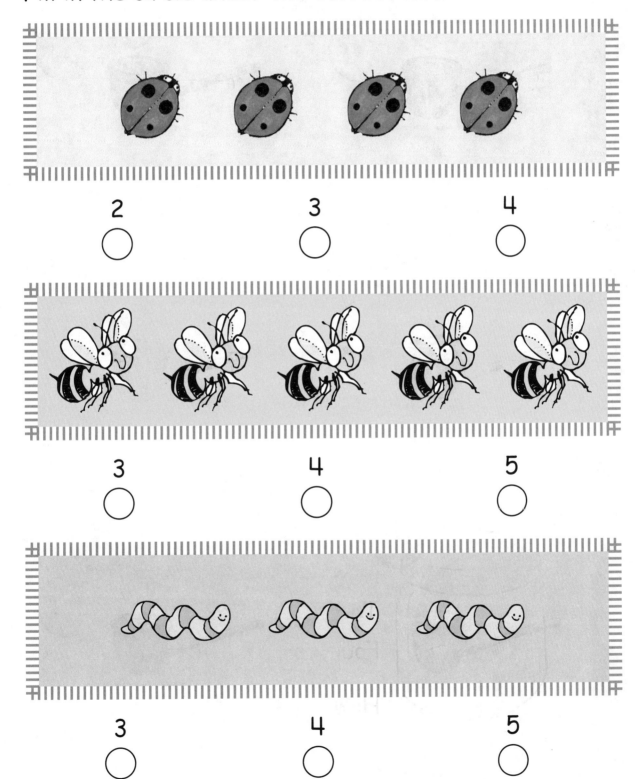

2   3   4
○   ○   ○

3   4   5
○   ○   ○

3   4   5
○   ○   ○

Blowing Bubbles

Count the bubbles. Write the number.

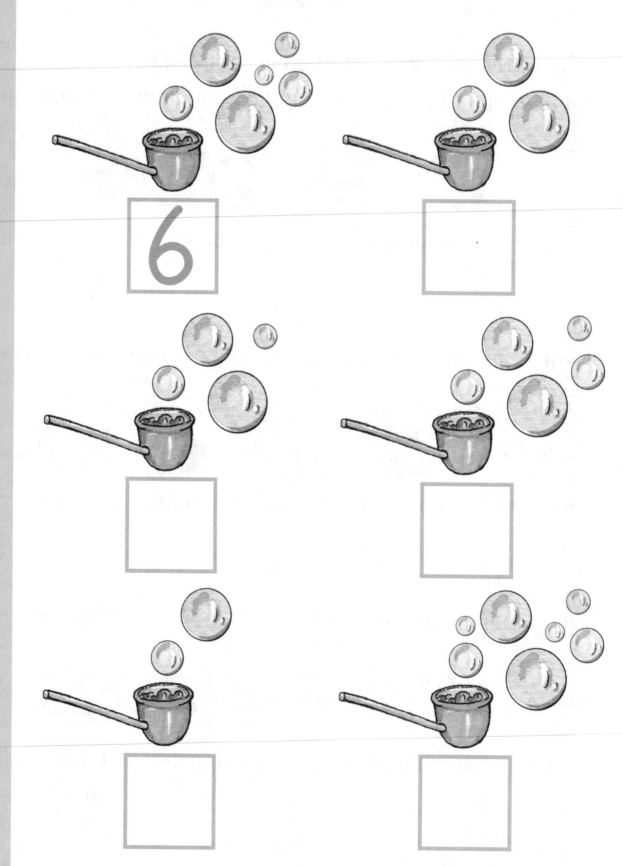

Skills:

Addition

Write the number.

$$3 + 3 = \underline{}$$

$$2 + 3 = \underline{}$$

$$3 + 2 = \underline{}$$

$$5 + 2 = \underline{}$$

$$3 + 1 = \underline{}$$

$$5 + 1 = \underline{}$$

Bubbles and Balls

Bunches of Balloons

Skills:

One-to-One
Correspondence

Counting

Writing
Numbers

Draw one balloon on each string.

Color the balloons.

Count the balloons.

Write the number.

UNIT 3

Sharpen Your Skills—Math • EMC 9718 • © Evan-Moor Corp.

Skills:

Word Problems

Comparing Sets

Josh and Sam play marbles.

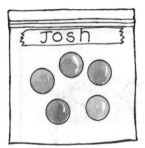 

Who has more marbles?

Josh   Sam

How many more? _____

Sally and Hope blow bubbles.
Sally blows three bubbles.
Hope blows five bubbles.

Who blew more bubbles?

Sally   Hope

How many more? _____

Bubbles and Balls

What Do You Think?

About how many balls are in each box?

Circle the correct number.

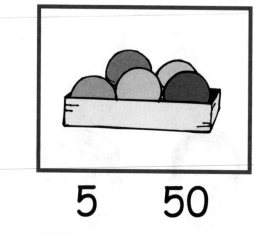

5   50

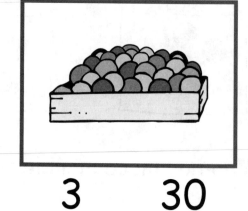

3   30

2   20

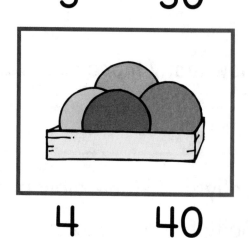

4   40

Draw 3 balls in the box.

Draw 6 balls in the box.

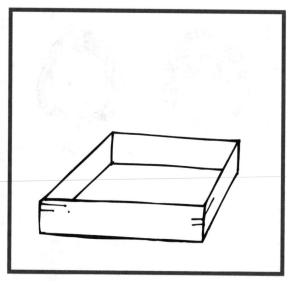

32

UNIT 3

Bubbles and Balls

Write the number.

3 popped.

Now there are ____2____.

$$\begin{array}{r} 5 \\ -3 \\ \hline \end{array}$$

2 popped.

Now there are _____.

$$\begin{array}{r} 4 \\ -2 \\ \hline \end{array}$$

1 popped.

Now there are _____.

$$\begin{array}{r} 3 \\ -1 \\ \hline \end{array}$$

4 popped.

Now there are _____.

$$\begin{array}{r} 6 \\ -4 \\ \hline \end{array}$$

2 popped.

Now there are _____.

$$\begin{array}{r} 2 \\ -2 \\ \hline \end{array}$$

Bubbles and Balls

Skills:

Patterning

Color the beads to finish the patterns.

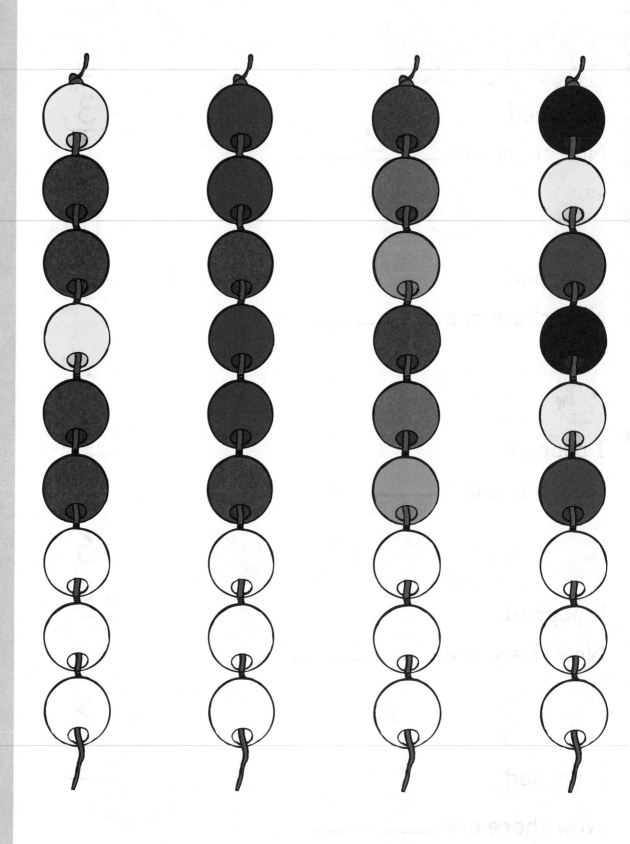

Bubbles and Balls

Cut and paste. Then write how many balls.

$\begin{array}{r} 1 \\ + 2 \\ \hline \end{array}$

paste

$\begin{array}{r} 3 \\ + 1 \\ \hline \end{array}$

paste

$\begin{array}{r} 4 \\ + 2 \\ \hline \end{array}$

paste

$\begin{array}{r} 2 \\ + 3 \\ \hline \end{array}$

paste

6 balls

5 balls

3 balls

4 balls

On the Scoreboard

Skills:

Word Problems: Addition

Comparing Numbers

Read and think. Write the number.

Jill scored 2 goals.

Molly scored 1 goal.

Syd scored 1 goal.

How many goals were scored in all?

Goals Scored

Jill:

Molly:

Syd:

Jesse scored 3 goals.

Todd scored 2 goals.

Abe scored 1 goal.

How many goals were scored in all?

Goals Scored

Jesse:

Todd:

Abe:

The Reds scored 5 goals.

The Blues scored 3 goals.

Who won? _____

By how much?

Bubbles and Balls

Great Gumballs!

Each gumball costs 1 penny.

Cut and paste to show how much each bag of gumballs costs.

paste	paste
paste	paste

paste	paste
paste	paste

paste	paste
paste	paste

paste	paste
paste	paste

The Balloon Man

Look at the balloons.

Count the different shapes.

Color one square for each balloon in the correct row.

Which shape has the most?

Which shape has the least?

Bubbles and Balls

Count the dots. Fill in the circle for the answer.

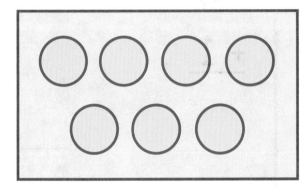

5   6   7   5   6   7

○ ○ ○   ○ ○ ○

About how many are in the box?
Fill in the circle for the answer.

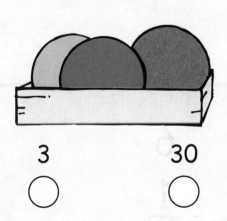

3   30   2   20

○   ○   ○   ○

Finish the pattern.

How Many Wheels?

Draw the wheels. Write the number.

2 + 3 5	4 + 1
3 + 3	5 + 2
1 + 2	6 + 1

Vehicles

Circle the one that is heavier.
Tell someone how you know.

Draw one that is heavier.

Vehicles

Here Comes the Train!

Count to tell how many cars the engine is pulling.
Write the number.

 _____

 _____

 _____

 _____

 _____

 _____

Vehicles

Skills:

Subtraction

Draw the pile. Write the number.

There were 6 boxes.

 If the takes  ,

how many will be left?

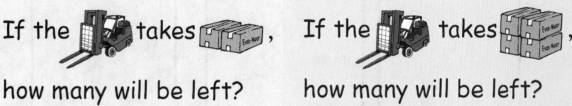 If the takes  ,

how many will be left?

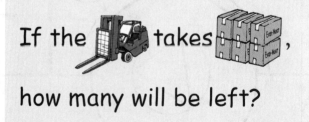 If the takes ,

how many will be left?

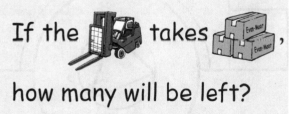 If the takes ,

how many will be left?

Vehicles

A Colorful Ride!

Color the shapes.

 = red = blue △ = yellow

Add a driver.

Write the number.

Skills:

Addition

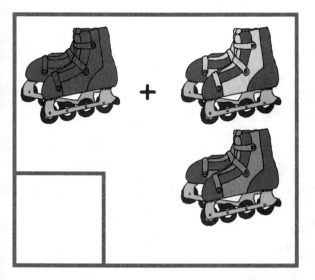

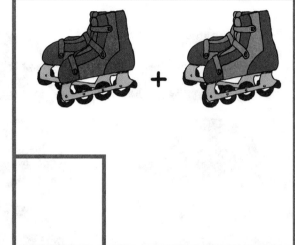

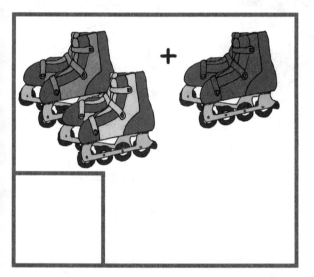

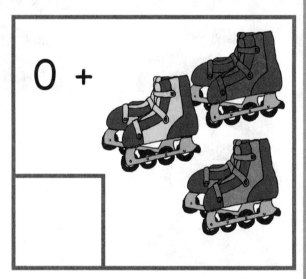

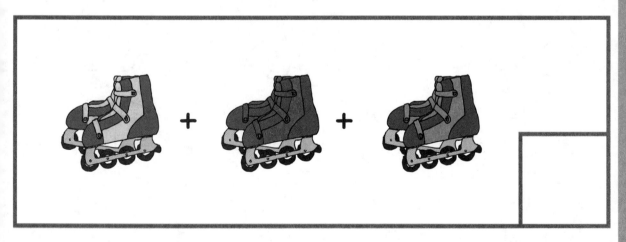

Vehicles

Make a Pattern

Color the cars to finish the patterns.

Skills:

Counting

Graphing

Count the wheels on each vehicle. Color a square in the row that tells the correct number of wheels.

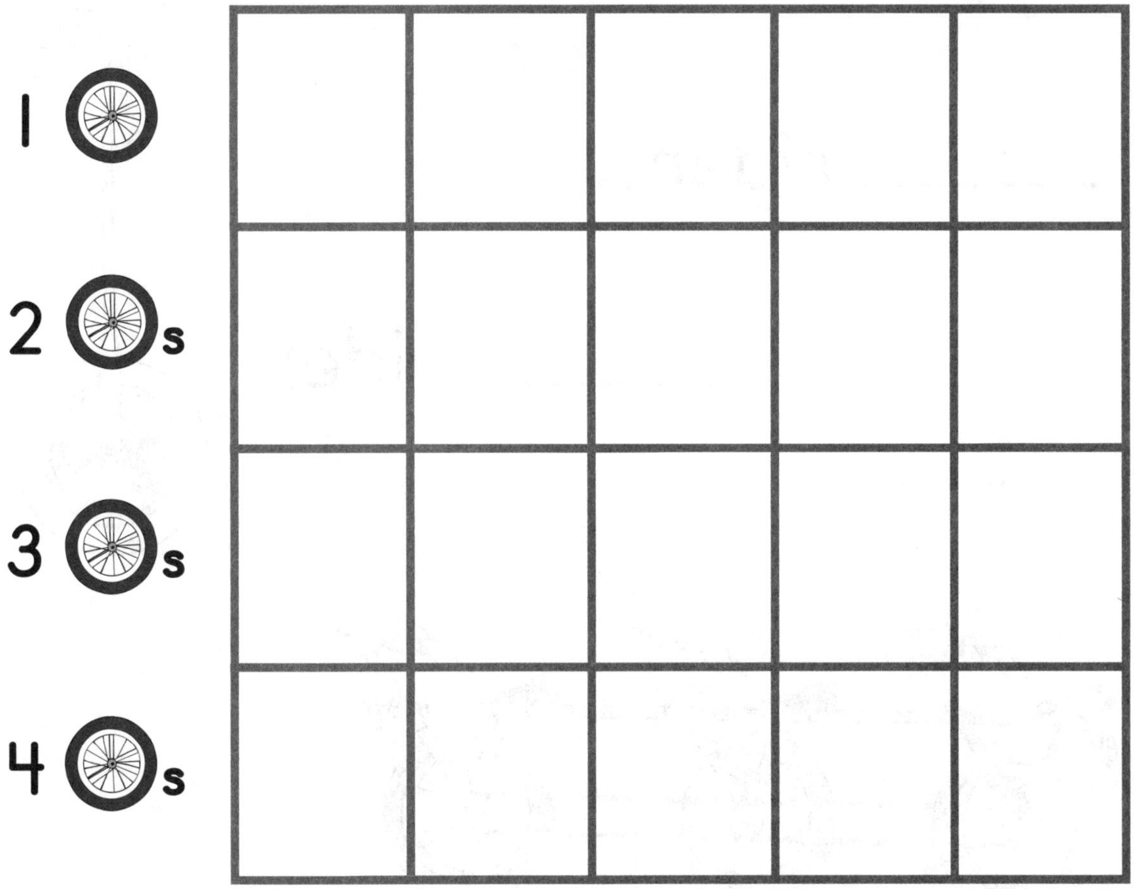

1 🛞

2 🛞s

3 🛞s

4 🛞s

Which row has the most vehicles? _____

Vehicles

Pedal It!

Skills:

One-to-One
Correspondence

Draw the riders. Put one on each seat.
Write the number.

_____ riders

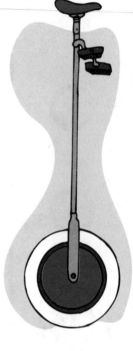

_____ rider

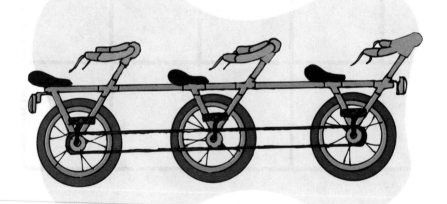

_____ riders

Vehicles

Skills:

Word
Problems:
Addition

Mom, Joy, John, and Jim got in.

Gramps climbed in, too.

How many are in the van? _____

Mark, Scottie, Josh,
and Max rode to school.

They picked up Tori
and Chelsea.

How many are in the van? _____

Jeff and Emma rode in
the van to the game.

They took four friends
with them.

How many are in the van? _____

Vehicles

New Cars

Cut and paste.

Put the cars on the .

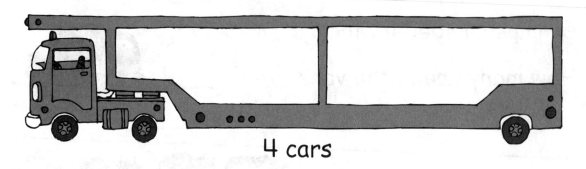

4 cars

6 cars

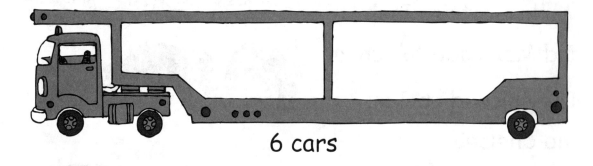

3 cars

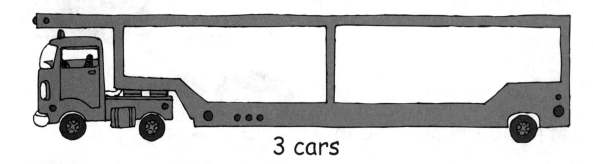

5 cars

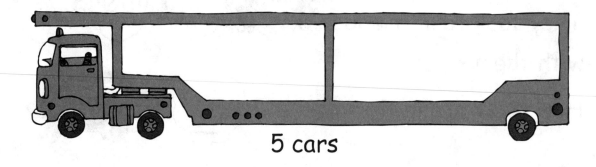

Skills:

Addition

Write the number.

 = _____

 = _____

 = _____

 = _____

 = _____

 = _____

 +0 = _____

 = _____

Vehicles

Tim has 2 balls.

Tom has 3 balls.

Who has more balls?

_____

Which is the heaviest?

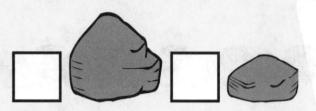

Draw the wheels. Add.

$$\begin{array}{r} 4 \\ + 3 \\ \hline \square \end{array}$$

$$\begin{array}{r} 2 \\ + 2 \\ \hline \square \end{array}$$

Finish the pattern.

Planting a Garden

Cut and paste.

Put one plant in each hole.

How many plants are growing?_____

How Many Ears of Corn?

Skills:

Counting

Comparing
Numbers

This is an ear of corn.

Circle the ears. Count them.

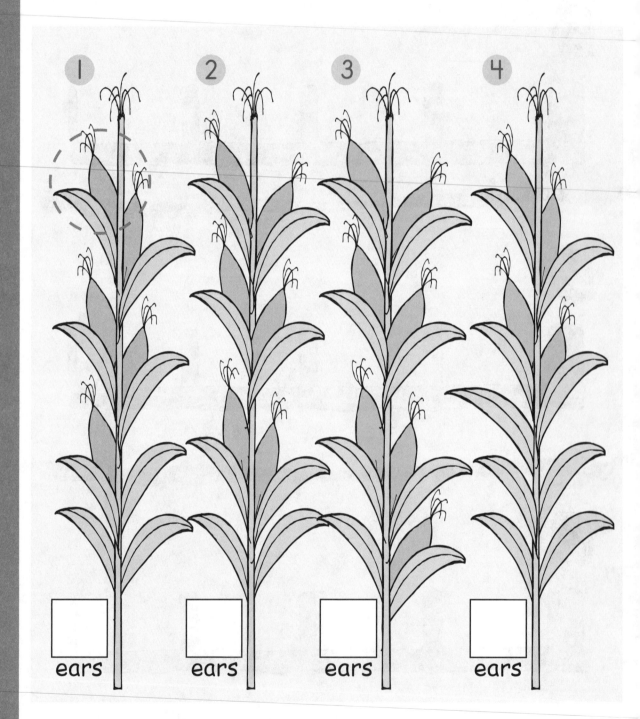

ears	ears	ears	ears

Which stalk has the most ears?　1　2　3　4

My Garden

Skills:

Addition

Draw the correct number. Then write how many in all.

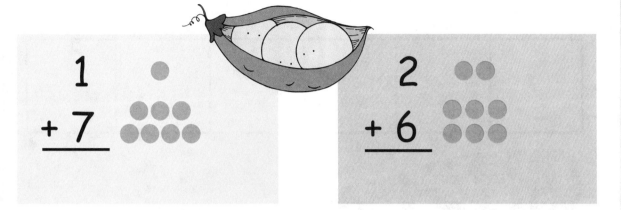

```
  1
+ 7
____
```

```
  2
+ 6
____
```

```
  3
+ 5
____
```

```
  4
+ 4
____
```

```
  5
+ 3
____
```

```
  6
+ 2
____
```

```
  7
+ 1
____
```

```
  8
+ 0
____
```

My Garden

How Long Is the Carrot?

Color the blocks purple to measure the carrot.

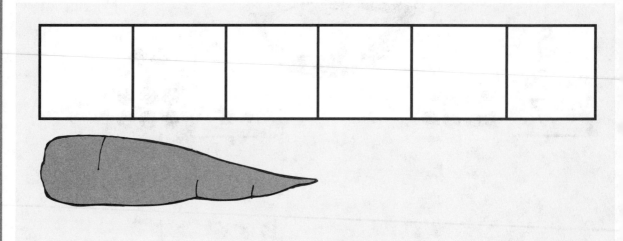

The carrot is _____ ▢ s long.

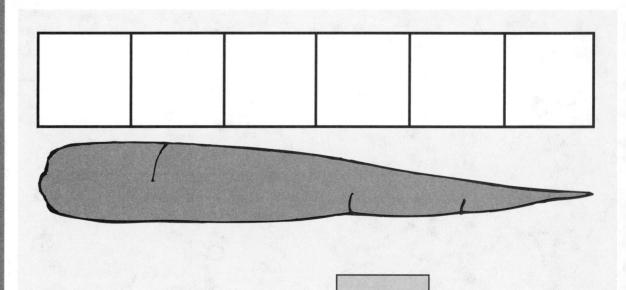

The carrot is _____ ▢ s long.

Skills:

Comparing Numbers

Counting by 5s

Count the plants in each row. Write the number.

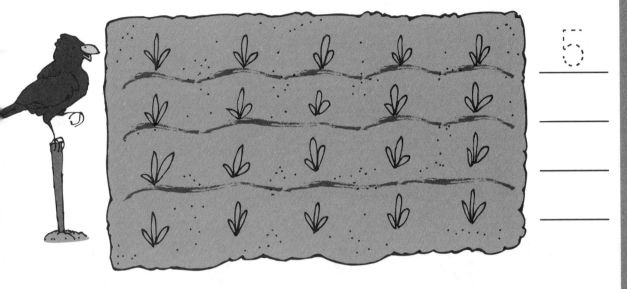

Are all the rows the same?   ◯ yes   ◯ no

5 10 15 20

Trace the big numbers. Count by 5s.

How many plants in all? _____

My Garden

What Will You Need?

Connect the dots to see something you will need for your garden. Start with 1.

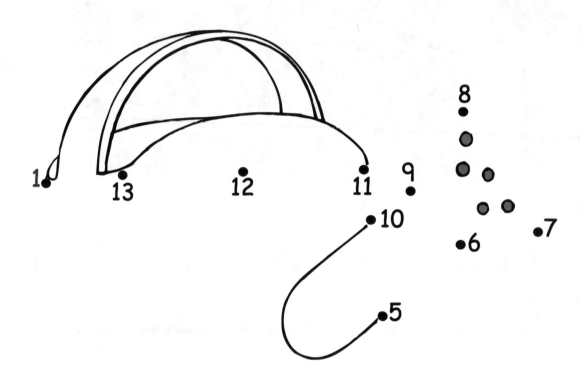

My Garden

How Many Are Left?

There were 8 carrots in the row.

Gramps picked 3.

How many are left?

There were 8 beets in the row.

Grammy picked 5.

How many are left?

There were 8 onions in the row.

Dad picked 4.

How many are left?

There were 8 turnips in the row.

Mom picked 6.

How many are left?

My Garden

Fill the Basket

Cut and paste the berries.

Put the correct number in each basket.

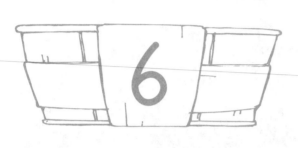

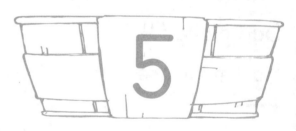

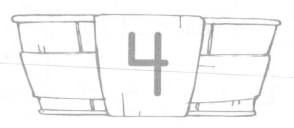

Sharpen Your Skills—Math • EMC 9718 • © Evan-Moor Corp.

Skills:

Addition

Draw the flowers. Then write the number.

$3 + 4 = \boxed{7}$

$2 + 2 = \boxed{}$

$1 + 5 = \boxed{}$

$4 + 2 = \boxed{}$

$5 + 2 = \boxed{}$

$3 + 3 = \boxed{}$

My Garden

Seeds to Plant

Look at the   .

Color in one square on the graph for each packet.

Count how many of each kind there are.

Most   Least

My Garden

How Many?

Add.

4 + 1 = _____

6 + 2 = _____

3 + 4 = _____

5 + 3 = _____

Subtract.

8 - 3 = _____

7 - 4 = _____

8 - 2 = _____

5 - 1 = _____

My Garden

TEST YOUR SKILLS

Count the dots. Write the number.

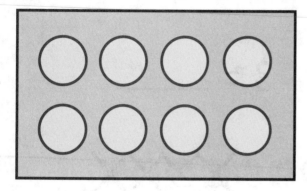

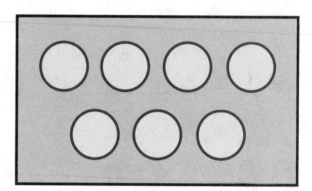

_____   _____

Fill in the circle for the answer.

4 + 4 = _____

6   7   8
○   ○   ○

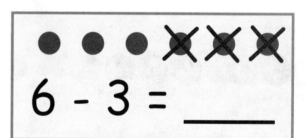

6 - 3 = _____

3   4   5
○   ○   ○

5 + 2 = _____

5   6   7
○   ○   ○

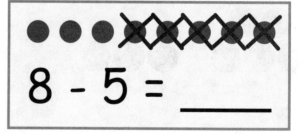

8 - 5 = _____

2   3   4
○   ○   ○

Color the fish. Count the fish. Write the numbers
to complete the number sentence.

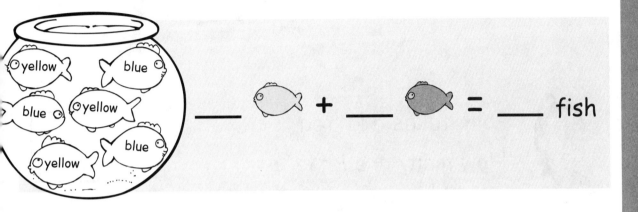

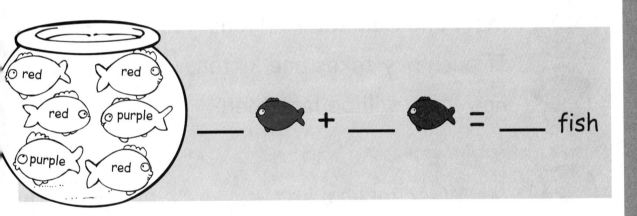

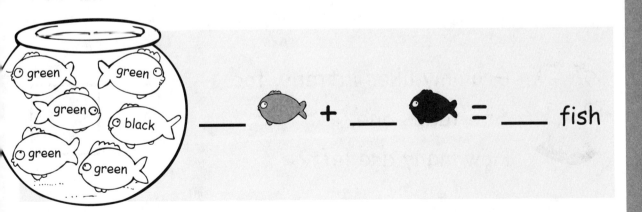

Fun with Pets

Five Kittens

Mother cat had five kittens.
The kittens need homes.

 Polly takes a kitten.
How many are left?

 Matt and Sam want kittens, too.
If each boy takes one kitten,
how many will be left then?

 Mr. West takes a kitten.
How many kittens are left?

 Grammy likes kittens, too.
She takes one.
How many are left?

Fun with Pets

Skills:

Comparing
Numbers

Circle the picture to tell which is more.

Which is more?

Which is more?

Which is more?

Which is more?

Which is more?

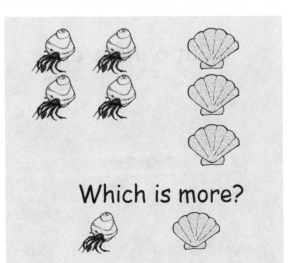

Which is more?

Fun with Pets

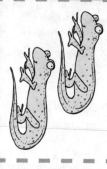
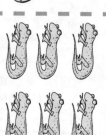

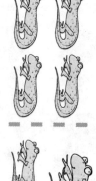

Read the numbers. Cut and paste.
Put the animals in their cages.

Put 4 in here.

paste

Put 3 in here.

paste

Put 5 in here.

paste

Put 2 in here.

paste

Put 6 in here.

paste

Put 1 in here.

paste

Skills:

Number Order

Spot wants to eat. Follow the dots to find his bone. Start with 1.

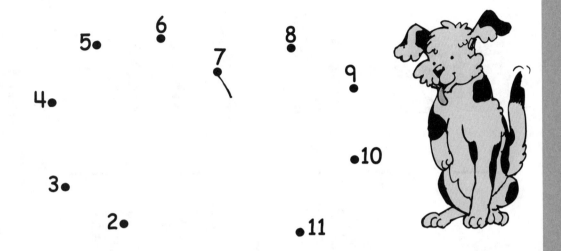

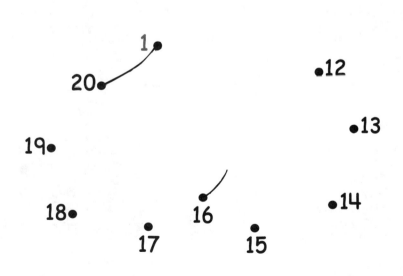

Fun with Pets

Cat Food on the Shelf

Skills:

Counting

Writing Numbers

Addition

Count the cans. Write the numbers.

Add to tell how many.

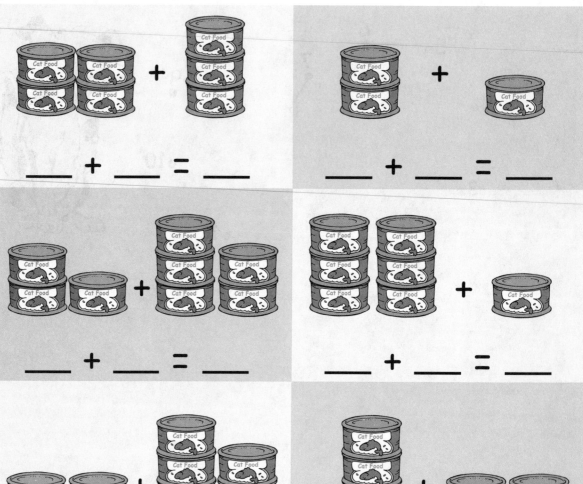

___ + ___ = ___

___ + ___ = ___

___ + ___ = ___

___ + ___ = ___

___ + ___ = ___

___ + ___ = ___

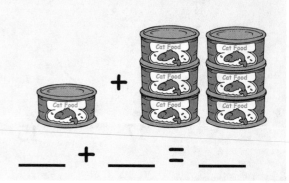

___ + ___ = ___

___ + ___ = ___

Skills:

Understanding Numbers

Addition

Draw the ants. Write the numbers.

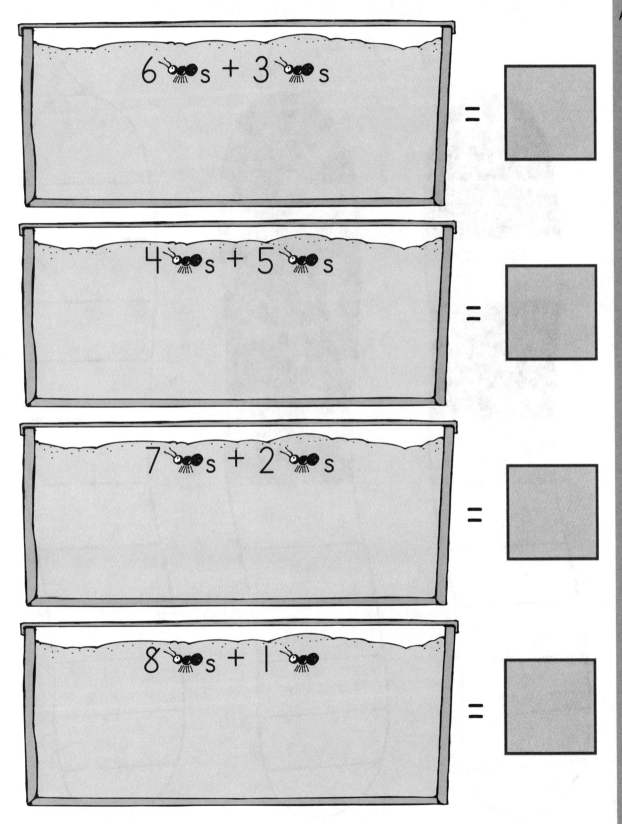

6 🐜s + 3 🐜s

=

4 🐜s + 5 🐜s

=

7 🐜s + 2 🐜s

=

8 🐜s + 1 🐜

=

Fun with Pets

See the Snakes!

Color the first 2 snakes in the patterns.
Make your own pattern for the third snake.

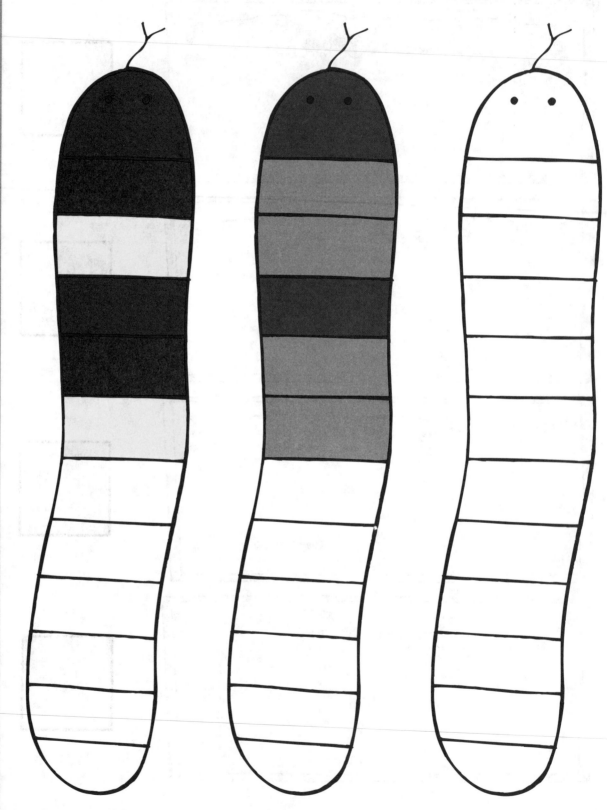

Sharpen Your Skills—Math • EMC 9718 • © Evan-Moor Corp.

Fun with Pets

Which Weighs More?

Look at the two pets in each box.

Color the one that weighs more.

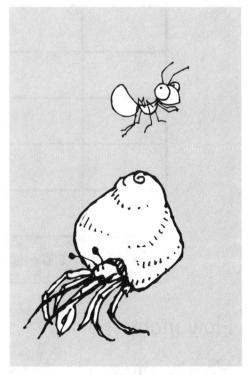

Fun with Pets

Here is a list of the pets at the pet store:

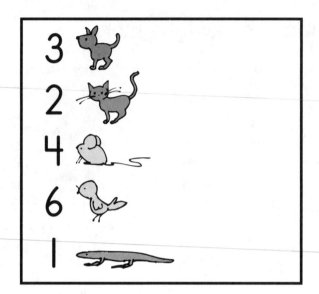

Color a square in the correct row for each animal.

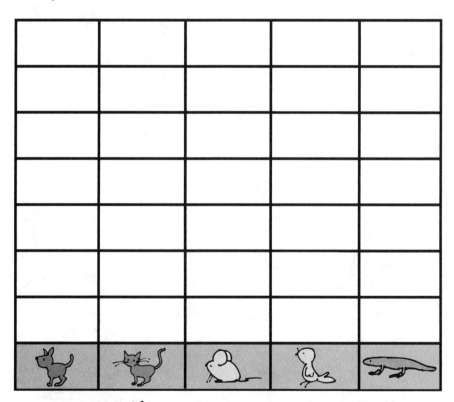

How many more 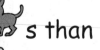s than s? _____

How many more s than s? _____

The Dog Show

Cut and paste. Put the dogs in order.

Start with 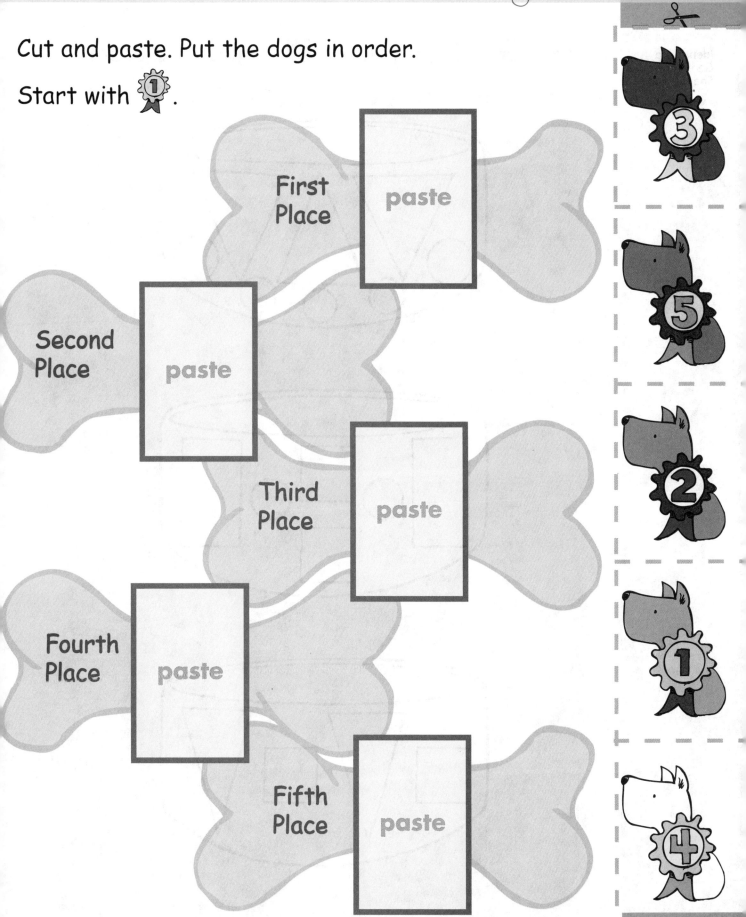.

First
Place

paste

Second
Place

paste

Third
Place

paste

Fourth
Place

paste

Fifth
Place

paste

Colorful Collars

Color: ● red △ yellow ■ purple ■ green

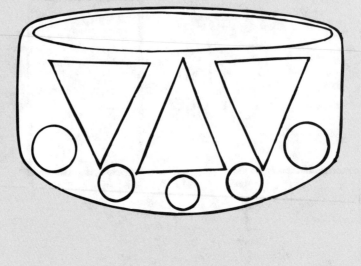

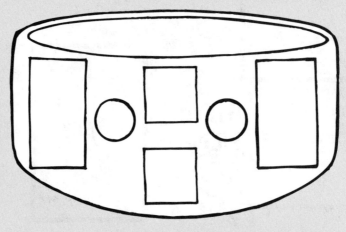

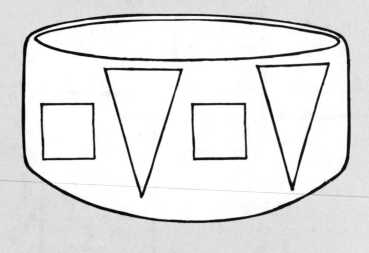

Fun with Pets

Draw dots and add.

$$5 \circ\circ\circ\circ\circ$$
$$+\, 3$$

$$4$$
$$+\, 4$$

Subtract.

$$5 - 1 = \underline{\qquad}$$

$$7 - 4 = \underline{\qquad}$$

Color the shapes.

● red   ■ yellow   ▲ blue

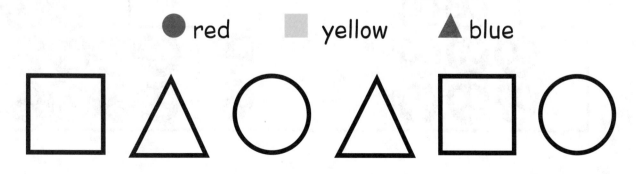

Practice writing these numbers.

6 6 6 7 7 7

8 8 8 9 9 9

10 10 10 10 10 10

Count the pretzels. Write how many.

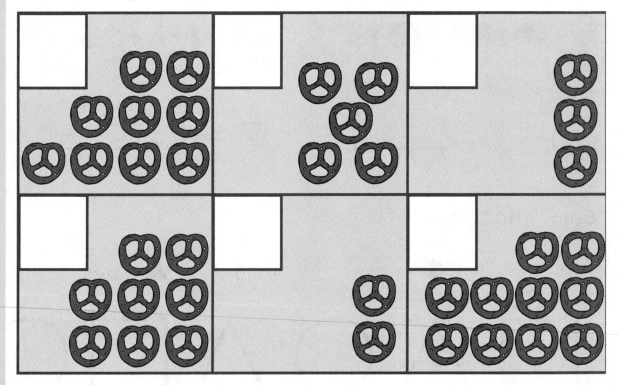

Snack Time

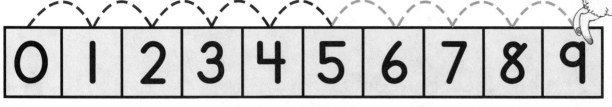

Hop 5 spaces. Hop 4 more spaces.

| 0 | 1 | 2 | 3 | 4 | 5 | 6 | 7 | 8 | 9 |

$5 + 4 = \underline{\quad}$

Skills:

Using a Number Line for Addition

Hop 6 spaces. Hop 3 more spaces.

| 0 | 1 | 2 | 3 | 4 | 5 | 6 | 7 | 8 | 9 |

$6 + 3 = \underline{\quad}$

Hop 2 spaces. Hop 7 more spaces.

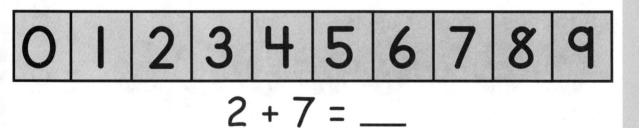

$2 + 7 = \underline{\quad}$

Hop 8 spaces. Hop 1 more space.

| 0 | 1 | 2 | 3 | 4 | 5 | 6 | 7 | 8 | 9 |

$8 + 1 = \underline{\quad}$

Snack Time

Eating Carrots

Cross out the carrot coins that are eaten.

Write how many are left.

Ann has 6 carrot coins.

She eats 2.

How many are left?

6
− 2

Ben has 5 carrot coins.

He eats 3.

How many are left?

5
− 3

Beth has 8 carrot coins.

She eats 6.

How many are left?

8
− 6

Tim has 7 carrot coins.

He eats 4.

How many are left?

7
− 4

Snack Time

Skills:
Fractions—$\frac{1}{2}$

Draw a line to divide the snacks in half.

Remember, the two pieces must be the same size.

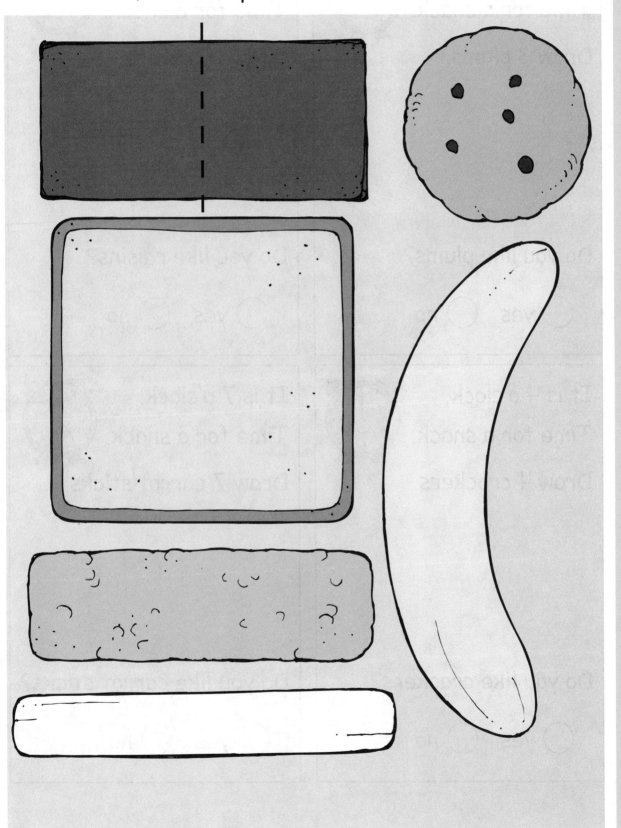

Snack Time

It is 3 o'clock.

Time for a snack.

Draw 3 plums.

Do you like plums?

◯ yes ◯ no

It is 10 o'clock.

Time for a snack.

Draw 10 raisins.

Do you like raisins?

◯ yes ◯ no

It is 4 o'clock.

Time for a snack.

Draw 4 crackers.

Do you like crackers?

◯ yes ◯ no

It is 7 o'clock.

Time for a snack.

Draw 7 carrot sticks.

Do you like carrot sticks?

◯ yes ◯ no

Snack Time

UNIT 7

Mrs. Tom's Day Care kids voted on their favorite fruit.

Here's a graph that shows how they voted.

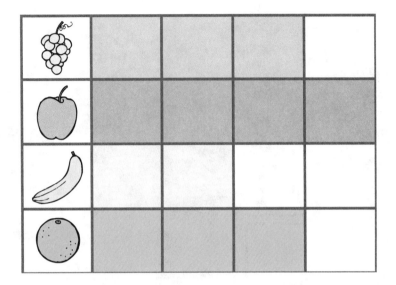

Which fruit got the most votes?

   (orange)

Which fruit got the fewest votes?

   (orange)

Which two fruits got the same number of votes?

   (orange)

Which fruit would you vote for?

   (orange)

Snack Time

How Many Nuts?

Draw the peanuts in the shells.

Then write the number to tell how many in all.

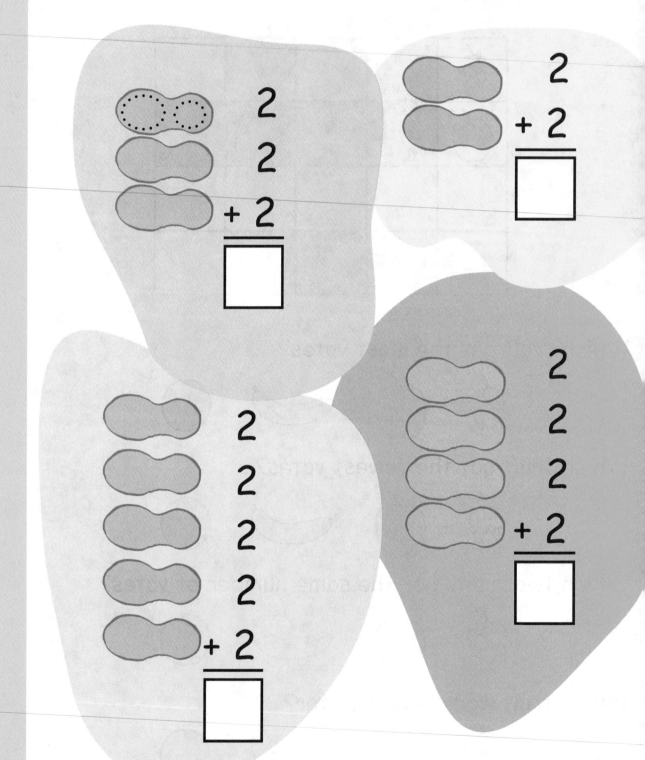

Snack Time

Sharpen Your Skills—Math • EMC 9718 • © Evan-Moor Corp.

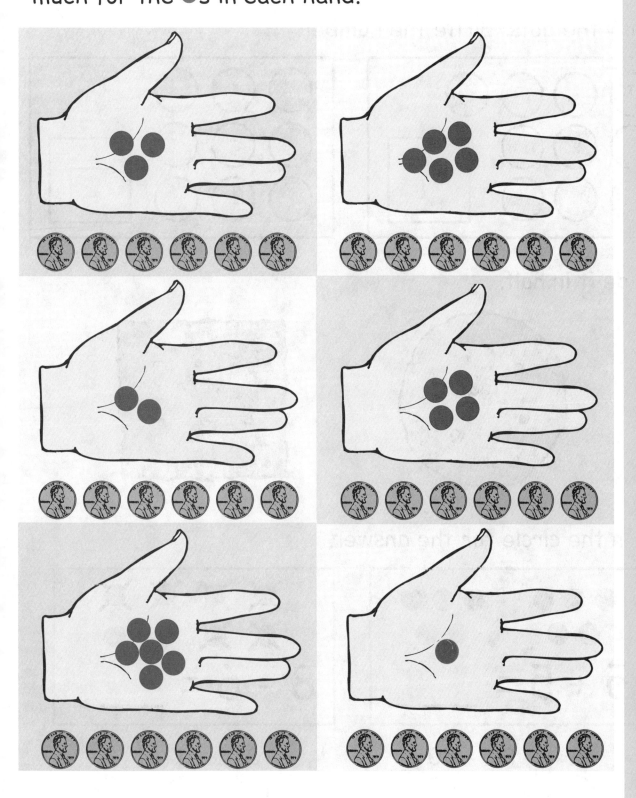

Each ● costs 1 cent. Circle the pennies to show how much for the ●s in each hand.

Count the dots. Write the number.

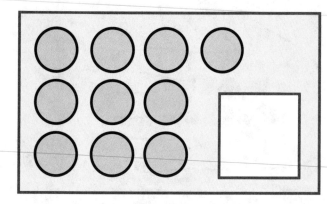 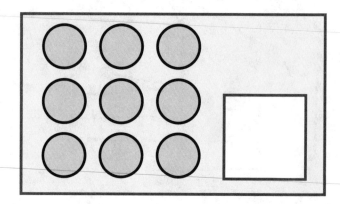

Divide it in half.

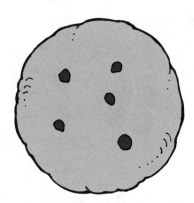 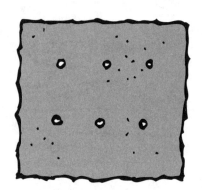

Fill in the circle for the answer.

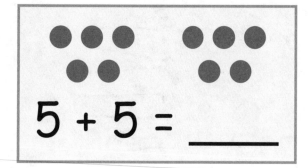

5 + 5 = _____

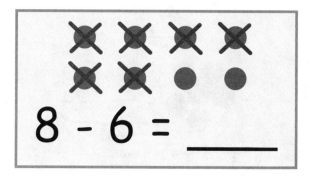

8 − 6 = _____

6   8   10
○   ○   ○

2   4   6
○   ○   ○

Answer Key

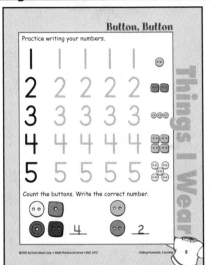

Button, Button

Practice writing your numbers.

1 | | | | |
2 2 2 2 2
3 3 3 3 3
4 4 4 4 4
5 5 5 5 5

Count the buttons. Write the correct number.

4   2

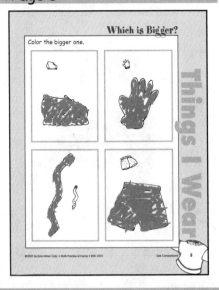

Adding 1

Draw one more. Count how many. Write the number.

+ = 2 (Draw)

+ Draw a hat. = 3

+ Draw a mitten. = 4

+ Draw a sock. = 5

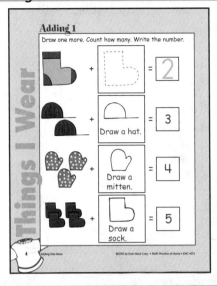

Which is Bigger?

Color the bigger one.

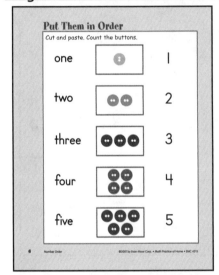

Put Them in Order

Cut and paste. Count the buttons.

one		1
two		2
three		3
four		4
five		5

Just One Hat

Color the hats. Draw a line from a 😊 to a 🎩.

Hats should be colored. Answers will vary.

Which has more? 🎩 😊

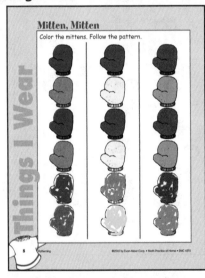

Mitten, Mitten

Color the mittens. Follow the pattern.

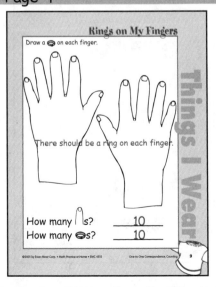

Rings on My Fingers

Draw a ⬭ on each finger.

There should be a ring on each finger.

How many ⟋s?   10
How many ⬭s?   10

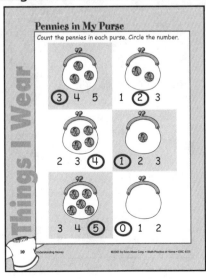

Pennies in My Purse

Count the pennies in each purse. Circle the number.

③ 4 5   1 ② 3
2 3 ④   ① 2 3
3 4 ⑤   ⓪ 1 2

What Is It?

Connect the dots. Start with 1.

Will 🐰 stay dry?   😊 yes   😞 no

© Evan-Moor Corp. • EMC 9718 • Sharpen Your Skills—Math

87

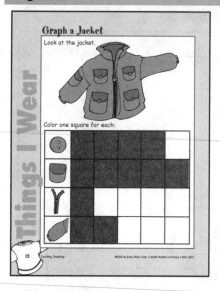

Graph a Jacket

Look at the jacket.

Color one square for each:

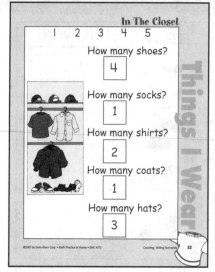

In The Closet

1 2 3 4 5

How many shoes? 4

How many socks? 1

How many shirts? 2

How many coats? 1

How many hats? 3

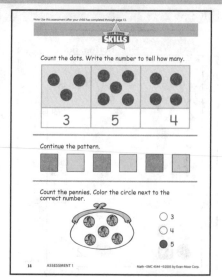

Note: Use this assessment after your child has completed through page 13.

SKILLS

Count the dots. Write the number to tell how many.

3   5   4

Continue the pattern.

Count the pennies. Color the circle next to the correct number.

○ 3
○ 4
● 5

Bugs, Bugs, Bugs

Count the bugs. Circle the number to tell how many.

1 2 ③ 4 5   ① 2 3 4 5   1 2 3 4 ⑤

① 2 3 4 5   1 2 ③ 4 5   ① 2 3 4 5

0 ② 3 4 5   ⓪ 1 2 3 4 5   0 1 2 3 ④ 5

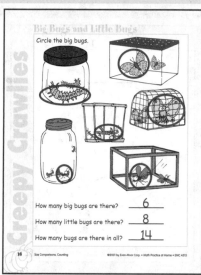

Big Bugs and Little Bugs

Circle the big bugs.

How many big bugs are there?   6

How many little bugs are there?   8

How many bugs are there in all?   14

A Bug Hunt

Tom put in one bug. Draw it. Juan put in two bugs. Draw them.

Maria put in two bugs. Draw them. Sue put in three bugs. Draw them.

There should be 3 bugs.

There should be 5 bugs.

How many bugs are in the jar? 3

How many bugs are in the box? 5

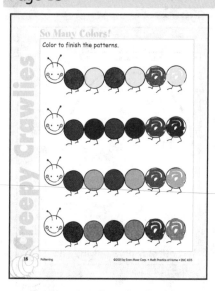

So Many Colors!

Color to finish the patterns.

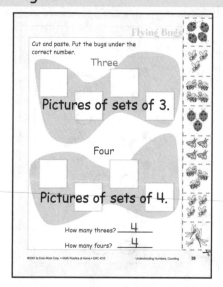

Flying Bugs

Cut and paste. Put the bugs under the correct number.

Three

Pictures of sets of 3.

Four

Pictures of sets of 4.

How many threes? 4

How many fours?   4

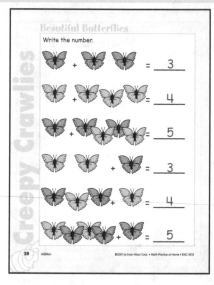

Beautiful Butterflies

Write the number.

+   = 3

+   = 4

+   = 5

+   = 3

+   = 4

+   = 5

Page 21

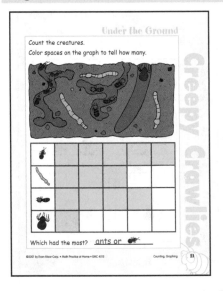

Under the Ground

Count the creatures.
Color spaces on the graph to tell how many.

Which had the most? ants or 🕷

Page 22

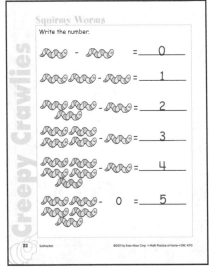

Squirmy Worms

Write the number.

〜 - 〜 = ___0___

〜 - 〜 = ___1___

〜 - 〜 = ___2___

〜 - 〜 = ___3___

〜 - 〜 = ___4___

〜 - 0 = ___5___

Page 23

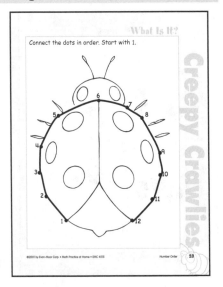

What Is It?

Connect the dots in order. Start with 1.

Page 24

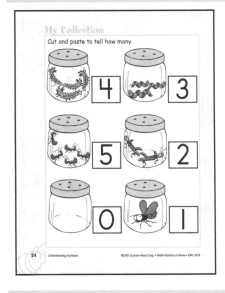

My Collection

Cut and paste to tell how many.

4   3
5   2
0   1

Page 25

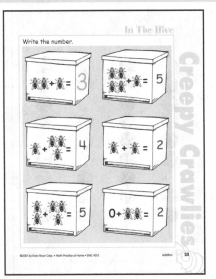

In The Hive

Write the number.

+ = 3   + = 5
+ = 4   + = 2
+ = 5   0+ = 2

Page 26

They Got Away

Matt had five ladybugs in his jar.
The lid came off.
Five ladybugs got out.
How many are left?   0

Mandy had three ants in her jar.
The lid came off.
Three ants got out.
How many are left?   0

Max had four worms in his jar.
The lid came off.
Four worms got out.
How many are left?   0

Page 27

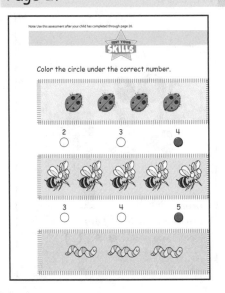

Note: Use this assessment after your child has completed through page 26.

TEST YOUR SKILLS

Color the circle under the correct number.

2   3   4
○   ○   ●

3   4   5
○   ○   ●

Page 28

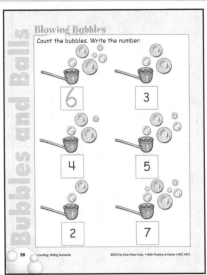

Blowing Bubbles

Count the bubbles. Write the number.

6   3
4   5
2   7

Page 29

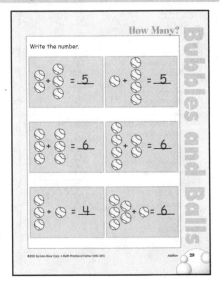

How Many?

Write the number.

+ = _5_   + = _5_
+ = _6_   + = _6_
+ = _4_   + = _6_

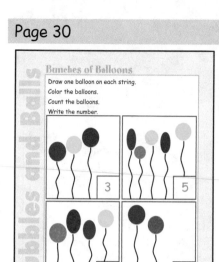

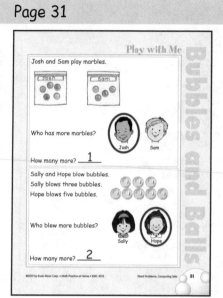

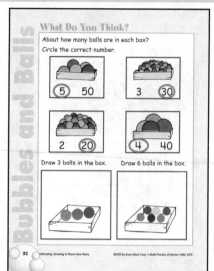

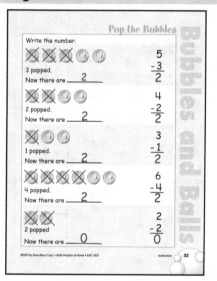

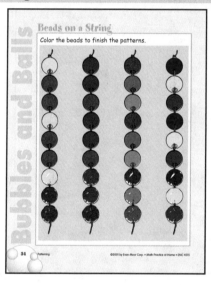

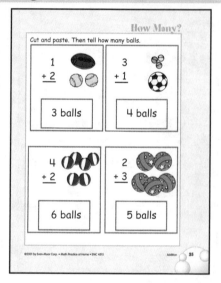

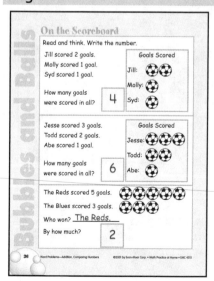

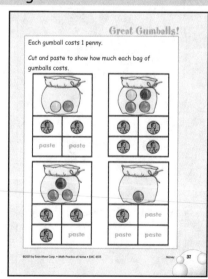

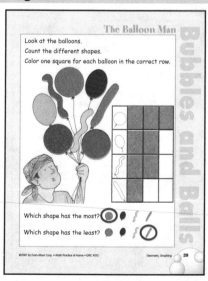

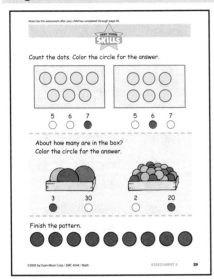

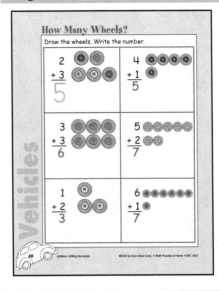

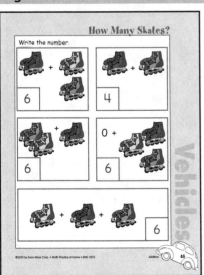

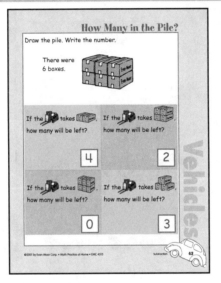

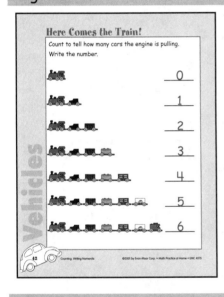

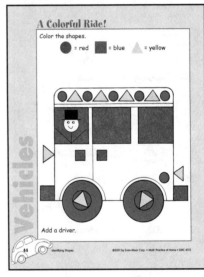

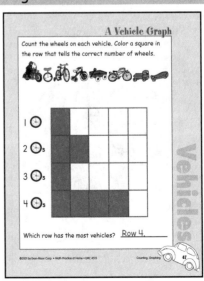

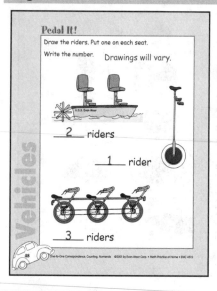

Pedal It!

Draw the riders. Put one on each seat.

Write the number.   Drawings will vary.

2 riders

1 rider

3 riders

How Many in the Van?

Mom, Joy, John, and Jim got in.
Gramps climbed in, too.
How many are in the van? 5

Mark, Scottie, Josh,
and Max rode to school.
They picked up Tori
and Chelsea.
How many are in the van? 6

Jeff and Emma rode in
the van to the game.
They took four friends
with them.
How many are in the van? 6

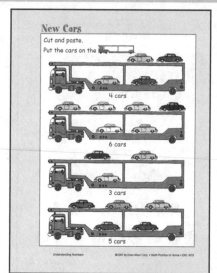

New Cars

Cut and paste.
Put the cars on the...

4 cars

6 cars

3 cars

5 cars

How Many?

Write the number.

🚗🚗🚗🚗 + 🚗🚗🚗 = 7

🚙🚙🚙🚙🚙🚙 + 🚙 = 7

🚗🚗🚗🚗🚗 + 🚗🚗 = 7

🚙🚙🚙 + 🚙🚙🚙🚙 = 7

🚗🚗 + 🚗🚗🚗🚗🚗 = 7

🚙🚙🚙🚙🚙🚙🚙 + 0 = 7

🚗🚗🚗🚗🚗🚗🚗 + 🚗🚗🚗 = 6

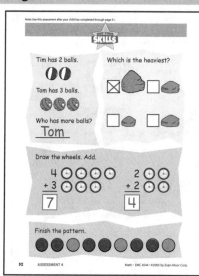

SKILLS

Tim has 2 balls.

Tom has 3 balls.

Who has more balls?
Tom

Which is the heaviest?

Draw the wheels. Add.

$\begin{array}{r}4\\+3\\\hline 7\end{array}$ $\begin{array}{r}2\\+2\\\hline 4\end{array}$

Finish the pattern.

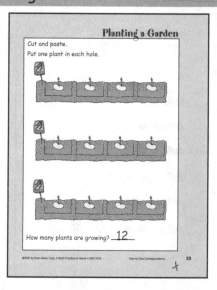

Planting a Garden

Cut and paste.
Put one plant in each hole.

How many plants are growing? 12

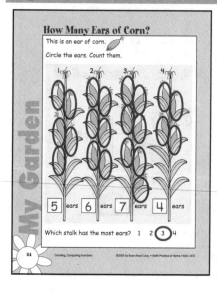

How Many Ears of Corn?

This is an ear of corn.

Circle the ears. Count them.

1   2   3   4

5 ears   6 ears   7 ears   4 ears

Which stalk has the most ears?   1   2   ③   4

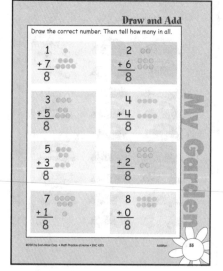

Draw and Add

Draw the correct number. Then tell how many in all.

$\begin{array}{r}1\\+7\\\hline 8\end{array}$ $\begin{array}{r}2\\+6\\\hline 8\end{array}$

$\begin{array}{r}3\\+5\\\hline 8\end{array}$ $\begin{array}{r}4\\+4\\\hline 8\end{array}$

$\begin{array}{r}5\\+3\\\hline 8\end{array}$ $\begin{array}{r}6\\+2\\\hline 8\end{array}$

$\begin{array}{r}7\\+1\\\hline 8\end{array}$ $\begin{array}{r}8\\+0\\\hline 8\end{array}$

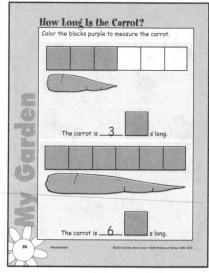

How Long Is the Carrot?

Color the blocks purple to measure the carrot.

The carrot is 3 s long.

The carrot is 6 s long.

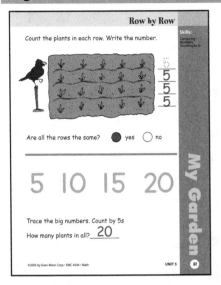

Row by Row

Count the plants in each row. Write the number.

5
5
5

Are all the rows the same? ● yes ○ no

5 10 15 20

Trace the big numbers. Count by 5s
How many plants in all? __20__

UNIT 5

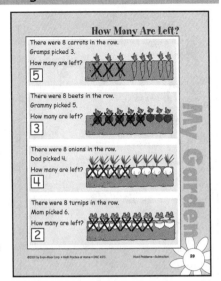

What Will You Need?

Connect the dots to see something you will need for your garden. Start with 1.

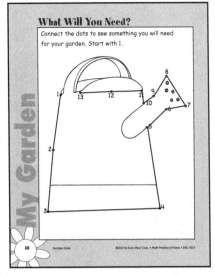

How Many Are Left?

There were 8 carrots in the row.
Gramps picked 3.
How many are left? |5|

There were 8 beets in the row.
Grammy picked 5.
How many are left? |3|

There were 8 onions in the row.
Dad picked 4.
How many are left? |4|

There were 8 turnips in the row.
Mom picked 6.
How many are left? |2|

Fill the Basket

Cut and paste the berries.
Put the correct number in each basket.

6
3
8
5
2
4

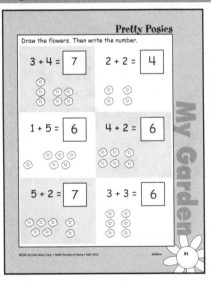

Pretty Posies

Draw the flowers. Then write the number.

$3 + 4 = 7$

$2 + 2 = 4$

$1 + 5 = 6$

$4 + 2 = 6$

$5 + 2 = 7$

$3 + 3 = 6$

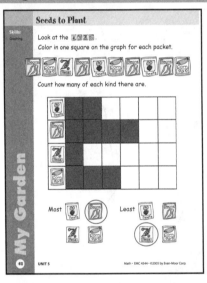

Seeds to Plant

Look at the seeds.
Color in one square on the graph for each packet.

Count how many of each kind there are.

Most _____ Least _____

How Many?

Add.

$4 + 1 = 5$

$6 + 2 = 8$

$3 + 4 = 7$

$5 + 3 = 8$

Subtract.

$8 - 3 = 5$

$7 - 4 = 3$

$8 - 2 = 6$

$5 - 1 = 4$

Note: Use this assessment after your child has completed through page 63.

SKILLS

Count the dots. Write the number.

8

7

Color the circle for the answer.

$4 + 4 = 8$
6 7 ●8

$6 - 3 = 3$
●3 4 5

$5 + 2 = 7$
5 6 ●7

$8 - 5 = 3$
2 ●3 4

ASSESSMENT 5

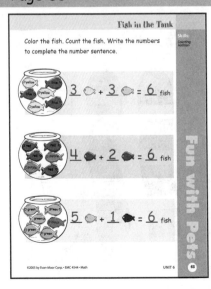

Fish in the Tank

Color the fish. Count the fish. Write the numbers to complete the number sentence.

$3 + 3 = 6$ fish

$4 + 2 = 6$ fish

$5 + 1 = 6$ fish

UNIT 6

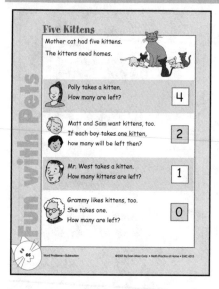

Five Kittens

Mother cat had five kittens.

The kittens need homes.

Fun with Pets

Polly takes a kitten.
How many are left? **4**

Matt and Sam want kittens, too.
If each boy takes one kitten,
how many will be left then? **2**

Mr. West takes a kitten.
How many kittens are left? **1**

Grammy likes kittens, too.
She takes one.
How many are left? **0**

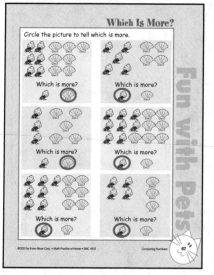

Which Is More?

Circle the picture to tell which is more.

Which is more?   Which is more?

Which is more?   Which is more?

Which is more?   Which is more?

Fun with Pets

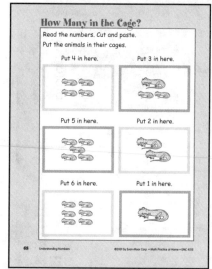

How Many in the Cage?

Read the numbers. Cut and paste.
Put the animals in their cages.

Put 4 in here.   Put 3 in here.

Put 5 in here.   Put 2 in here.

Put 6 in here.   Put 1 in here.

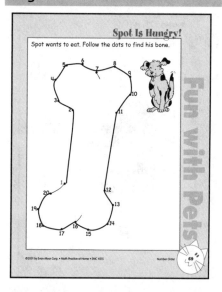

Spot Is Hungry!

Spot wants to eat. Follow the dots to find his bone.

Fun with Pets

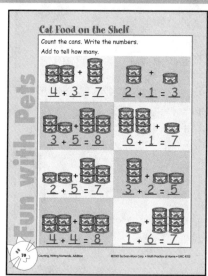

Cat Food on the Shelf

Count the cans. Write the numbers.
Add to tell how many.

$4 + 3 = 7$ $2 + 1 = 3$

$3 + 5 = 8$ $6 + 1 = 7$

$2 + 5 = 7$ $3 + 2 = 5$

$4 + 4 = 8$ $1 + 6 = 7$

Fun with Pets

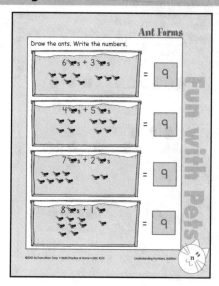

Ant Farms

Draw the ants. Write the numbers.

6 s $+ 3$ s $= 9$

4 s $+ 5$ s $= 9$

7 s $+ 2$ s $= 9$

8 s $+ 1$ s $= 9$

Fun with Pets

See the Snakes!

Color the first 2 snakes in the patterns.

Make your own pattern.

Pattern
will vary

Fun with Pets

Which Weighs More?

Look at the two pets in each box.
Color the one that weighs more.

Fun with Pets

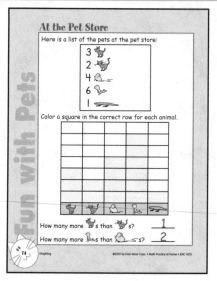

At the Pet Store

Here is a list of the pets at the pet store:

3
2
4
6
1

Color a square in the correct row for each animal.

How many more s than s?   **1**

How many more s than s?   **2**

Fun with Pets

94

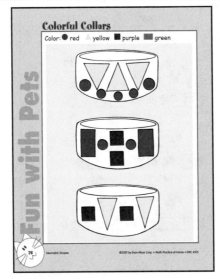

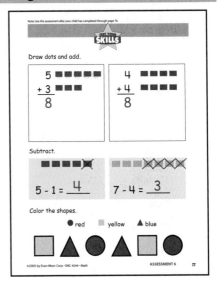

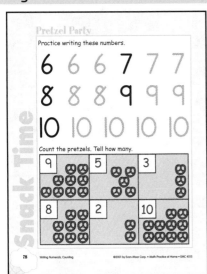

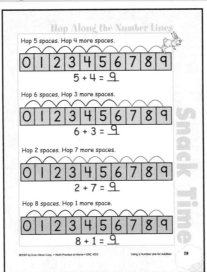

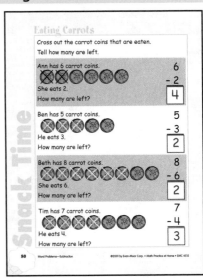

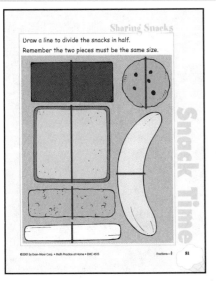

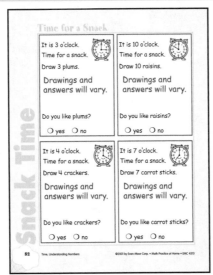

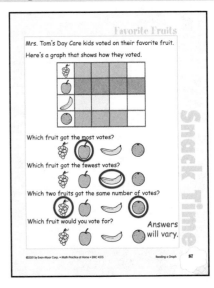

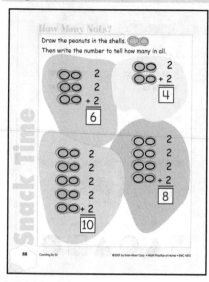

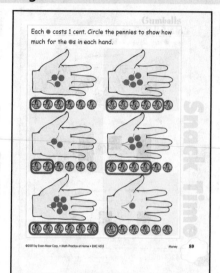

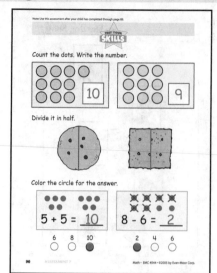

Contents

A Fat Cat

A fat cat sat.

A fat cat sat on a mat.

Read the spelling words.
Check off the words you can find in the story.

☐ cat   ☐ mat   ☐ sat

Skills:

Spelling Words in the **at** Word Family

Visual Memory

Fine Motor Skills

Spelling Practice

Read and Spell	Trace and Spell	Trace and Spell
1. cat	cat	cat
2. sat	sat	sat
3. mat	mat	mat

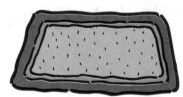

cat   sat   mat

My Spelling Words

Color the cat.

Write the correct word to complete each sentence.

1. The _____ sat on a mat.

2. The cat _____ on a mat.

3. The cat sat on a _____ .

| mat | sat | cat |

What Is Missing?

Write the missing letters.

c__t   ma__   __at

ca__   m__t   s__t

__at   __at   sa__

Write a sentence about the cat.

_____

_____

It Rhymes with  at

Write **at** to spell each word.

c __ __

m __ __

h __ __

b __ __

r __ __

p __ __

Skills:

Word Meaning

Using Picture
Clues

Identifying
Like Words

Make a Match

Draw a line to make a match.

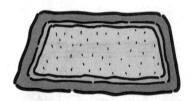

sat

mat

cat

Circle the word that is the same as the first word.

mat	cat	mat	fat
cat	fat	cat	mat
fat	fat	mat	cat

More Than One

Add **s** to a word to show more than one.

cat

cat _s__

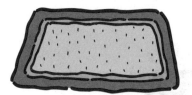

mat

mat_____

bat

bat_____

hat

hat_____

Skills:

Completing
Sentences
with Spelling
Words

Using Picture
Clues

The Cat

Write the missing word to complete each sentence.

cat   sat   mat

1. The cat _____.

2. The _____ ran.

3. The cat's _____ is red.

My Cat

Color the picture.

Write the sentence in the correct order.

on	the mat.	sat	Cat

_____

_____

A Fat Cat

My Spelling Test

Find the correct answer.
Fill in the circle.

1. Which word is spelled correctly?
   ○ kat
   ○ cat

2. Which word is spelled correctly?
   ○ mat
   ○ mut

3. Which word means more than one bat?
   ○ bats
   ○ bat

4. Which word means more than one hat?
   ○ hat
   ○ hats

1. _____

2. _____

3. _____

Sharpen Your Skills—Spell & Write • EMC 9718 • © Evan-Moor Corp.

Pup

Did Pup hop?

Pup did hop to the top.

Did Mom mop?

Mom did mop.

Find It!

Read the spelling words.
Check off the words you can find in the story.

___ mop   ___ hop   ___ top

Skills:

Spelling Words in the **op** Word Family

Visual Memory

Fine Motor Skills

Spelling Practice

Read and Spell	Trace and Spell	Trace and Spell
1. hop	hop	hop
2. top	top	top
3. mop	mop	mop

hop

top

mop

My Spelling Words

Color the pup.

Write the correct word to complete each sentence.

Did the pup _____?

The pup did hop on _____.

The pup did not _____.

top	hop	mop

What Is Missing?

Write the missing letters.

h__p   mo__   t__p

ho__   m__p   __op

__op   __op   to__

Write a sentence about who can hop.

_____

_____

It Rhymes with **op**

Write **op** to spell each word.

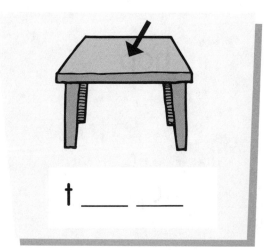

t ___ ___

m ___ ___

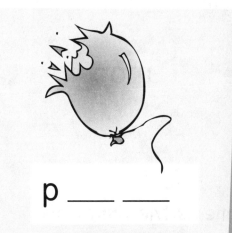

p ___ ___

h ___ ___

st ___ ___

sh ___ ___

Skills:

Word Meaning

Using Picture
Clues

Identifying
Like Words

Make a Match

Draw a line to make a match.

hop

top

mop

Circle the word that is the same as the first word.

hop	mop	hop	top
top	top	hop	mop
mop	top	mop	hop

Ask or Tell?

Ask: Did the cat hop?

Tell: The cat did hop.

Write a **.** or a **?** to complete each sentence.

1. Did Pup hop____

2. Pup did hop____

3. Mom did mop____

4. Did Mom mop____

Finish the pictures. Draw.

Pup is on top.

Mom did mop.

Skills:

Completing
Sentences
with Spelling
Words

Using Picture
Clues

See Pup

Write the missing word to complete each sentence.

mop	hop	top

1. Can the pup _____?

2. Is the pup on _____?

3. Did the pup _____?

A Funny Frog

Look at the picture.

Write the sentence in the correct order.

hops	on	Frog	the log.

_____

_____

 **Pup**

My Spelling Test

Find the correct answer.
Fill in the circle.

1. Which word is spelled correctly?

　○ hop
　○ hup

2. Which word is spelled correctly?

　○ mot
　○ mop

3. Does the sentence ask or tell?

　Mom did mop ＿＿＿

　○ tell
　○ ask

4. Does the sentence ask or tell?

　Pup did hop＿＿＿

　○ tell
　○ ask

1. ＿＿＿＿＿＿＿

2. ＿＿＿＿＿＿＿

3. ＿＿＿＿＿＿＿

Pin It

Put the pin in.

Will you win?

Put the pin in.

You did win!

 **Find It!**

Read the spelling words.
Check off the words you can find in the story.

⬜ pin ⬜ in ⬜ win

Skills:

Spelling Words in the **in** Word Family

Visual Memory

Fine Motor Skills

Spelling Practice

Read and Spell	Trace and Spell	Trace and Spell
1. in	in	in
2. pin	pin	pin
3. win	win	win

in   pin   win

My Spelling Words

Color the picture.

Write the correct word to complete each sentence.

1. She did _____ it in to win.

2. She did pin it _____ to win.

3. She did pin it in to _____.

| pin | in | win |

What Is Missing?

Write the missing letters.

i___   pi___   w___n

___n   p___n   wi___

   ___in   ___in

Write a sentence about what is in the box.

_____

_____

It Rhymes with **in**

Write **in** to spell each word.

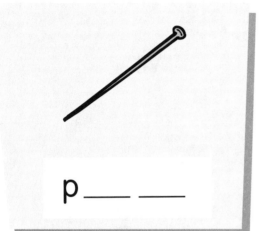

p ___ ___

sp ___ ___

f ___ ___

t ___ ___ can

w ___ ___

tw ___ ___

Skills:

Word Meaning

Using Picture
Clues

Identifying
Like Words

Make a Match

Draw a line to make a match.

win

pin

in

Circle the word that is the same as the first word.

win	win	pin	in
in	pin	in	win
pin	in	win	pin

Make a Sentence

A sentence is a group of words that tell a complete idea. The first part of a sentence tells <u>who</u>, the second part tells <u>what</u>.

Who: **Ben**
What: **can jump**

Ben can jump.

Draw a line to make a sentence.

Ben   did win.

Sam   can jump.

Kim   can pin it.

Ann   runs fast.

Skills:

Completing
Sentences
with Spelling
Words

Using Picture
Clues

Pat

Write the missing word to complete each sentence.

pin	in	win

1. Is Pat _____ it?

2. Can Pat _____ it?

3. Pat will _____ it on.

The Pup

Look at the picture.

Write the sentence in the correct order.

pup	win.	will	The

_____

_____

Note: Read the questions for your child. Then say each word *(in, pin, win)* for your child to write on the spelling test.

Pin It

My Spelling Test

Find the correct answer.
Fill in the circle.

1. Which word is spelled correctly?

   ○ wen
   ○ win

2. Which word rhymes with **in**?

   ○ pan
   ○ pin

3. Which is a sentence?

   ○ he did.
   ○ He did win.

4. Which is a sentence?

   ○ Sam can jump.
   ○ Can jump.

1. _____

2. _____

3. _____

Fun in the Sun

Come run.

Come run in the sun.

It will be fun.

 **Find It!** Read the spelling words.
Check off the words you can find in the story.

☐ run ☐ fun ☐ sun

Skills:

Spelling Words in the **un** Word Family

Visual Memory

Fine Motor Skills

Spelling Practice

Read and Spell	Trace and Spell	Trace and Spell
1. fun	fun	fun
2. run	run	run
3. sun	sun	sun

fun   run   sun

My Spelling Words

Color the picture.

Write the correct word to complete each sentence.

1. It is _____ to run.

2. It is fun to _____.

3. It is fun to run in the _____.

| run | fun | sun |

What Is Missing?

Write the missing letters.

s__n   ru__   f__n

__un   __un   fu__

su__   r__n   __un

Write a sentence about the sun.

_____

_____

It Rhymes with

Write **un** to spell each word.

s ___ ___

f ___ ___

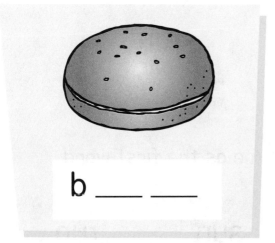

b ___ ___

r ___ ___

Skills:

Word Meaning

Using Picture
Clues

Identifying
Like Words

Make a Match

Draw a line to make a match.

fun

sun

run

Circle the word that is the same as the first word.

sun	fun	sun	run
fun	run	sun	fun
run	sun	run	fun

Names

A person's name always begins with a capital letter.

Ted   Lisa   Tom

Write the missing letter in each name.

 ___am

 ___at

 ___ed

 ___nn

 ___im

 ___ob

Write your name.

_____

Run, Pat, Run

Write the missing word to complete each sentence.

fun   sun   run

1. Pat can _____.

2. It is _____ to run in the sun.

3. Pat had fun running in the _____.

Run in the Sun

Look at the picture.

Write the sentence in the correct order.

in the sun.	to run	It is	fun

_____

_____

TEST YOUR SKILLS — Fun in the Sun

My Spelling Test

Find the correct answer.
Fill in the circle.

1. _____

1. Which word is spelled correctly?

○ san

2. _____

○ sun

2. Which word rhymes with **sun**?

3. _____

○ bun

○ bin

3. Which name begins correctly?

○ Sam

○ sam

4. Which name begins correctly?

○ bob

○ Bob

Red Hen

See the hen.

The hen is in a pen.

See the nest.

See ten eggs in the nest.

Find It!

Read the spelling words.
Check off the words you can find in the story.

| | ten | | hen | | pen |

Spelling Practice

Read and Spell	Trace and Spell	Trace and Spell
1. ten	ten	ten
2. hen	hen	hen
3. pen	pen	pen

ten   hen   pen

Skills:

Spelling Words in the **en** Word Family

Visual Memory

Fine Motor Skills

My Spelling Words

Color the picture.

Write the correct word to complete each sentence.

1. A big _____ is in the pen.

2. A big hen is in the _____.

3. A big hen sees _____.

pen   ten   hen

What Is Missing?

Write the missing letters.

he___	t___n	pe___
h___n	___en	___en
___en	te___	p___n

Write a sentence about the hen.

_____

_____

It Rhymes with

Write en to spell each word.

t _____ _____

m _____ _____

h _____ _____

d _____ _____

B _____ _____

p _____ _____

Skills:

Word Meaning

Using Picture
Clues

Identifying
Like Words

Make a Match

Draw a line to make a match.

pen

hen

ten

Circle the word that is the same as the first word.

ten	hen	ten	pen
pen	pen	ten	hen
hen	ten	pen	hen

More Than One

Add **s** to a word to show more than one.

hen

hen<u>s</u>

pen

pen_____

dog

dog_____

cow

cow_____

My Pet Hen

Write the missing word to complete each sentence.

| pen | ten | hen |

1. My _____ is red.

2. My hen has _____ eggs.

3. My hen is in a _____ .

Ten Hens

Look at the picture.

Write the sentence in the correct order.

hens	in the pen.	ten	See

_____

_____

Red Hen

My Spelling Test

Find the correct answer.
Fill in the circle.

1. Which word is spelled correctly?
   - ○ hin
   - ○ hen

2. Does **hen** rhyme with **pen**?
   - ○ yes
   - ○ no

3. Which word means more than one hen?
   - ○ hens
   - ○ hen

4. Which word means more than one den?
   - ○ den
   - ○ dens

1. _____

2. _____

3. _____

Stan and the Man

Stan got the can.

Stan ran.

Can the man get Stan?

Yes, he can.

 **Find It!**

Read the spelling words.
Check off the words you can find in the story.

___ can   ___ man   ___ ran

Spelling Practice

Read and Spell	Trace and Spell	Trace and Spell
1. ran	ran	ran
2. man	man	man
3. can	can	can

ran   man   can

My Spelling Words

Color the picture.

Write the correct word to complete each sentence.

1. The man had a _____.

2. The dog _____ to the man.

3. The _____ fed the dog.

| can | ran | man |

What Is Missing?

Write the missing letters.

___an	c___n	ra___
m___n	ca___	___an
ma___	___an	r___n

Write a sentence about the man.

_____

_____

It Rhymes with an

Write **an** to spell each word.

c____ ____

m____ ____

v____ ____

p____ ____

St____ ____

f____ ____

Skills:

Word Meaning

Using Picture
Clues

Identifying
Like Words

Make a Match

Draw a line to make a match.

can

man

ran

Circle the word that is the same as the first word.

man	can	man	ran
can	can	ran	man
ran	man	can	ran

Skills:

Using
Correct End
Punctuation

Comprehension

Ask or Tell?

Ask: Did the man run?

Tell: The man did run.

Write a **.** or a **?** to complete each sentence.

1. Did the man get Stan____

2. Did the dog run____

3. The man fed Stan____

4. Stan is a dog____

Draw.

The dog ran.	The man did <u>not</u> run.

Skills:

Completing
Sentences
with Spelling
Words

Using Picture
Clues

Stan Ran

Write the missing word to complete each sentence.

| Stan | man | ran | can |

1. Stan _____.

2. The _____ ran to get Stan.

3. The man got a _____.

4. The man fed _____.

Dan's Pups

Look at the picture.

Write the sentence in the correct order.

ran	to the can.	The pups

_____

_____

TEST YOUR SKILLS — Stan and the Man

My Spelling Test

Find the correct answer.
Fill in the circle.

1. _____

1. Which word is spelled correctly?

   ○ kan
   ○ can

2. _____

2. Does **can** rhyme with **Stan**?

   ○ yes
   ○ no

3. _____

3. Does the sentence ask or tell?

   Did the man run**?**

   ○ ask
   ○ tell

4. Does the sentence ask or tell?

   The dog ran**.**

   ○ ask
   ○ tell

Note: Read this story with your child. Ask: *Why does Dad have mitts on his hands?* Provide any help he or she needs to complete the tasks in this unit.

A Hot Pot

Is the pot hot?

It is hot.

Dad got the hot pot.

Read the spelling words.
Check off the words you can find in the story.

| ⌐ pot | ⌐ got | ⌐ hot |

Skills:

Spelling Words in the **ot** Word Family

Visual Memory

Fine Motor Skills

Spelling Practice

Read and Spell	Trace and Spell	Trace and Spell
1. hot	hot	hot
2. pot	pot	pot
3. got	got	got

hot   pot   got

My Spelling Words

Color the picture.

Write the correct word to complete each sentence.

1. Did Dad get the _____?

2. Dad _____ the pot.

3. The pot is not _____.

| got | hot | pot |

What Is Missing?

Write the missing letters.

__ot   ho__   g__t

p__t   h__t   go__

po__   __ot   __ot

Write a sentence about the hot pot.

_____

_____

It Rhymes with **ot**

Write **ot** to spell each word.

p___ ___

h___ ___

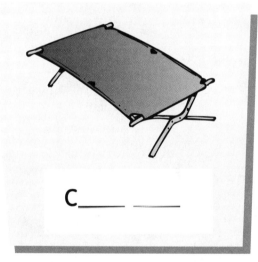

c___ ___

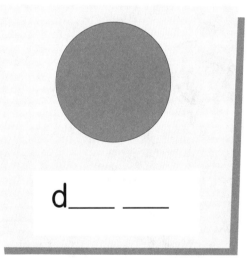

d___ ___

Skills:

Word Meaning

Using Picture
Clues

Identifying
Like Words

Make a Match

Draw a line to make a match.

got

hot

pot

Circle the word that is the same as the first word.

got	pot	got	hot
hot	hot	pot	got
pot	got	hot	pot

Capital Letters

The first word in a sentence begins with a capital letter.

The pot is hot.

Draw a line to make a match.

n   T

p   N

t   P

Write the capital letter to complete each sentence.

1.   p   ___ut it in the pot.

2.   t   ___he pot is hot.

3.   n   ___an got the pot.

Skills:

Completing
Sentences
with Spelling
Words

Using Picture
Clues

Kim

Write the missing word to complete each sentence.

hot   got   pot

1. Kim _____ an egg.

2. Kim put it in a _____.

3. The pot is _____.

It Is Hot!

Look at the picture.

Write the sentence in the correct order.

the hot pot.	got	The man

_____

_____

A Hot Pot

My Spelling Test

Find the correct answer.
Fill in the circle.

1. Which word is spelled correctly?

   ○ het
   ○ hot

2. Is the pot hot?

   ○ yes
   ○ no

3. Which sentence begins correctly?

   ○ dad got it.
   ○ Dad got it.

4. Which sentence begins correctly?

   ○ Get the pot.
   ○ get the pot.

1. _____

2. _____

3. _____

Note: Read this story with your child. Ask: *What did the pig dig up?* Provide any help he or she needs to complete the tasks in this unit.

A Big Pig

See the big pig.
See the pig dig.

Stop, pig, stop!
Do not dig!

Read the spelling words.
Check off the words you can find in the story.

___ pig   ___ dig   ___ big

Spelling Practice

Read and Spell	Trace and Spell	Trace and Spell
1. dig	dig	dig
2. pig	pig	pig
3. big	big	big

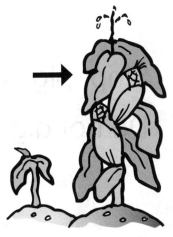

dig   pig   big

My Spelling Words

Skills:

Visual
Discrimination

Letter Order
in Words

Comprehension

Color the picture.

Write the correct word to complete each sentence.

1. See the big _____ dig in the mud.

2. See the _____ pig dig in the mud.

3. See the big pig _____ in the mud.

dig   pig   big

What Is Missing?

Write the missing letters.

p__g   bi__   d__g

pi__   b__g   __ig

__ig   __ig   di__

Write a sentence about the pig.

_____

_____

It Rhymes with **ig**

Write **ig** to spell each word.

p___ ___

d___ ___

w___ ___

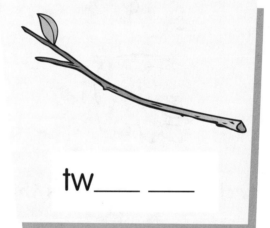

tw___ ___

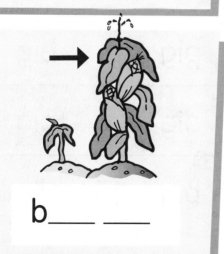

b___ ___

f___ ___

Make a Match

Draw a line to make a match.

pig

big

dig

Circle the word that is the same as the first word.

pig	dig	pig	big
big	big	dig	pig
dig	pig	big	dig

Name the Pigs

Write the missing letter to spell each pig's name.

B   D   J   P   S

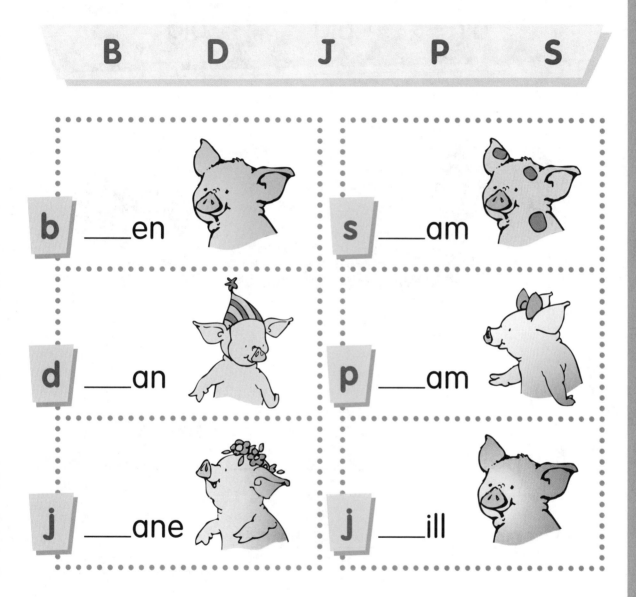

b   __en

s   __am

d   __an

p   __am

j   __ane

j   __ill

Write your name.

_____

Skills:

Completing
Sentences
with Spelling
Words

Using Picture
Clues

Pet Pig

Write the missing word to complete each sentence.

dig　　　pig　　　big

1. My pet pig is _____.

2. My pet pig can _____.

3. My pet _____ can run.

In the Pigpen

Look at the picture.

Write the sentence in the correct order.

the big pig	dig?	Did

_____

_____

TEST YOUR SKILLS — A Big Pig

My Spelling Test

Find the correct answer.
Fill in the circle.

1. _____

1. Which word is spelled correctly?

   ○ dig
   ○ dag

2. _____

2. Which name begins correctly?

   ○ Pam
   ○ pam

3. _____

3. Which name begins correctly?

   ○ dan
   ○ Dan

4. Did the pig in the story dig?

   ○ yes
   ○ no

Bad Sam

This is my pet Sam.

Will my pet get wet?

Sam is wet.
I am wet, too.

Find It!

Read the spelling words.
Check off the words you can find in the story.

☐ wet   ☐ pet   ☐ get

Skills:

Spelling Words in the **et** Word Family

Visual Memory

Fine Motor Skills

Spelling Practice

Read and Spell	Trace and Spell	Trace and Spell
1. get	get	get
2. pet	pet	pet
3. wet	wet	wet

get   pet   wet

My Spelling Words

Skills:

Visual
Discrimination

Letter Order
in Words

Comprehension

Color the picture.

Write the correct word to complete each sentence.

1. Did my _____ get wet?

2. Did I _____ wet?

3. My pet and I did get _____.

wet   pet   get

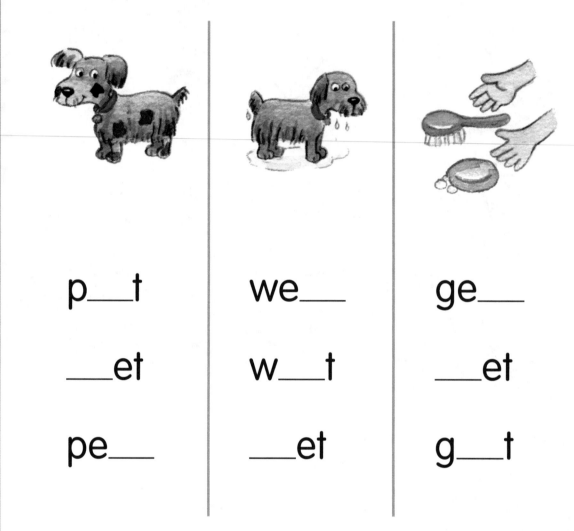

What Is Missing?

Write the missing letters.

p__t

__et

pe__

we__

w__t

__et

ge__

__et

g__t

Write a sentence about the wet pet.

_____

_____

It Rhymes with  et

Write **et** to spell each word.

j __ __

w __ __

m __ __

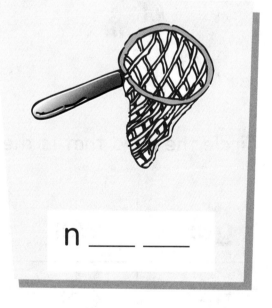

n __ __

Skills:

Word Meaning

Using Picture
Clues

Identifying
Like Words

Make a Match

Draw a line to make a match.

wet

pet

get

Circle the word that is the same as the first word.

get	wet	get	pet
pet	get	pet	wet
wet	pet	get	wet

What Did It Do?

A sentence is a group of words that tell a complete idea.
The first part of a sentence tells <u>who</u>, the second part
tells <u>what</u>.

> **Who: The pet cat**
> **What: had a nap**
>
> **The pet cat had a nap.**

Draw a line to make a sentence.

1. The pet cat   did dig.

2. The pet pig   can hop.

3. The wet frog   had a nap.

Skills:

Completing
Sentences
with Spelling
Words

Using Picture
Clues

Jan's Pet Cat

Write the missing word to complete each sentence.

wet   pet   get

1. Can Jan _____ her pet cat?

2. Jan's pet cat got _____.

3. Jan did get her _____ cat.

My Wet Pet

Look at the picture.

Write the sentence in the correct order.

and	did get wet.	a pet	A boy

_____

_____

Bad Sam

My Spelling Test

Find the correct answer.
Fill in the circle.

1. _____

1. Which word is spelled correctly?

   ○ pyt
   ○ pet

2. _____

2. Which word rhymes with **pet**?

   ○ get
   ○ hot

3. _____

3. Which one makes a sentence?

   The pet cat _____

   ○ had a nap.
   ○ had

4. Which one makes a sentence?

   The pet pig _____

   ○ wanted
   ○ wanted to dig.

Go to Sleep

Fred is fed.

It is time for bed.

Fred's bed is red.

Find It!

Read the spelling words.
Check off the words you can find in the story.

☐ bed   ☐ red   ☐ fed

Skills:

Spelling Words in the **ed** Word Family

Visual Memory

Fine Motor Skills

Spelling Practice

Read and Spell	Trace and Spell	Trace and Spell
1. red	red	red
2. bed	bed	bed
3. fed	fed	fed

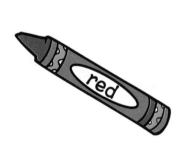

red

bed

fed

My Spelling Words

Color the picture.

Fred

Write the correct word to complete each sentence.

1. Fred was _____.

2. Fred is in _____.

3. Fred is in his _____ bed.

bed   fed   red

What Is Missing?

Write the missing letters.

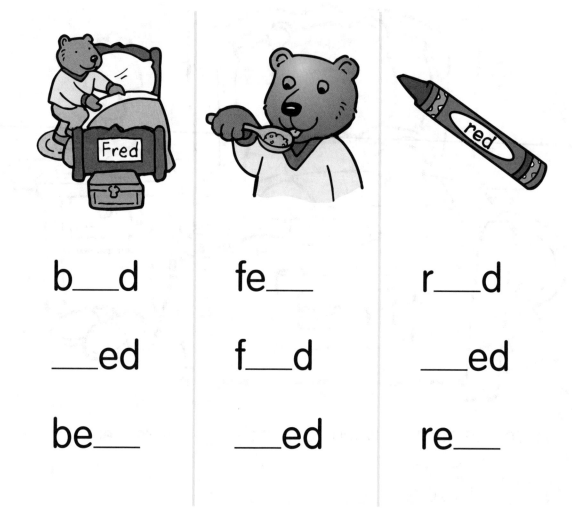

b__d   fe__   r__d

__ed   f__d   __ed

be__   __ed   re__

Write a sentence about the red bed.

_____

_____

It Rhymes with ed

Write **ed** to spell each word.

b ___ ___

f ___ ___

r ___ ___

w ___ ___

T ___ ___

sh ___ ___

Skills:

Word Meaning

Using Picture
Clues

Identifying
Like Words

Make a Match

Draw a line to make a match.

fed

bed

red

Circle the word that is the same as the first word.

bed	bed	fed	red
fed	red	bed	fed
red	fed	red	bed

Note: Remind your child that a sentence has two parts—who did something and what he or she did.

My Pet

Draw a line to make a **sentence**.

1. I fed   had a nap.

2. His bed   my pet.

3. My pet hamster   is red.

Write a **sentence** about your bed.

_____

_____

Who Did It?

Write the missing word to complete each sentence.

red	fed	bed

1. Mom _____ Fred.

2. Dad put Fred to _____.

3. Fred's bed is _____.

Bedtime

Look at the picture.

Write the sentence in the correct order.

is	the red bed.	in	Ted

_____

_____

Note: Read the questions for your child. Then say each spelling word *(fed, bed, red)* for your child to write on the spelling test.

TEST YOUR SKILLS — Go to Sleep

My Spelling Test

Find the correct answer.
Fill in the circle.

1. _____

1. Which word is spelled correctly?

   ◯ bed
   ◯ bede

2. _____

2. Which word rhymes with **Fred**?

   ◯ bed
   ◯ bad

3. _____

3. What color was Fred's bed?

   ◯ green
   ◯ red

4. Which one makes a sentence?

   Teddy is _____

   ◯ in the bed.
   ◯ in the

Note: Read this story with your child. Ask: *How did the bugs have fun?* Provide any help he or she needs to complete the tasks
in this unit.

1, 2, 3

1 bug.
1 bug dug.

2 bugs.
2 bugs hug.

3 bugs.
3 bugs tug.

Find It!

Read the spelling words.
Check off the words you can find in the story.

☐ bug   ☐ tug   ☐ dug

Skills:

Spelling Words in the **ug** Word Family

Visual Memory

Fine Motor Skills

Spelling Practice

Read and Spell	Trace and Spell	Trace and Spell
1. bug	bug	bug
2. tug	tug	tug
3. dug	dug	dug

bug

tug

dug

My Spelling Words

Color the picture.

Write the correct word to complete each sentence.

1. Ann _____ it up.

2. Ann had to _____ on the box.

3. A _____ is on the box.

bug   tug   dug

What Is Missing?

Write the missing letters.

b__g   t__g   du__

__ug   tu__   d__g

bu__   __ug   __ug

Write a sentence about a bug on a rug.

_____

_____

It Rhymes with  ug

Write **ug** to spell each word.

b ___ ___

r ___ ___

m ___ ___

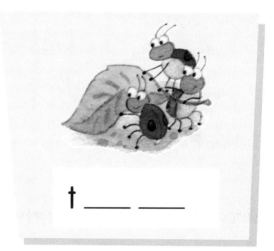

t ___ ___

h ___ ___

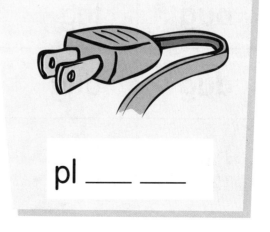

pl ___ ___

Skills:

Word Meaning

Using Picture
Clues

Identifying
Like Words

Make a Match

Draw a line to make a match.

tug

bug

dug

Circle the word that is the same as the first word.

bug	tug	bug	dug
dug	dug	bug	tug
tug	bug	tug	dug

More Than One

Add **s** to a word to show more than one.

bug   bugs

Look at the picture. Write the correct word.

bug   bug____

dog   dog____

mug   mug____

Skills:

Completing
Sentences
with Spelling
Words

Using Picture
Clues

A Bug

Write the missing word to complete each sentence.

hug	tug	bug

1. Will the _____ tug?

2. The bug will _____.

3. The bug will not _____.

Bug Fun

Look at the picture.

Write the sentence in the correct order.

dug	a fat bug.	up	Pat

_____

_____

TEST YOUR SKILLS 1, 2, 3

My Spelling Test

Find the correct answer.
Fill in the circle.

1. _____

1. Which word is spelled correctly?

   ○ dag
   ○ dug

2. _____

2. Which word rhymes with **bug**?

   ○ hug
   ○ tag

3. _____

3. Which word means more than one bug?

   ○ bugs
   ○ bug

4. Which word means more than one rug?

   ○ rug
   ○ rugs

T-Ball

Can I hit it?

I did hit it.

Now, I will sit.

Find It!

Read the spelling words.
Check off the words you can find in the story.

☑ hit   ☑ sit   ☑ it

Spelling Practice

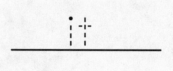

Read and Spell	Trace and Spell	Trace and Spell
1. it	it	it
2. sit	sit	sit
3. hit	hit	hit

it   sit   hit

My Spelling Words

Color the picture.

Write the correct word to complete each sentence.

1. Did she _____ it?

2. She did hit _____.

3. Will she _____ or run?

| it | hit | sit |

What Is Missing?

Write the missing letters.

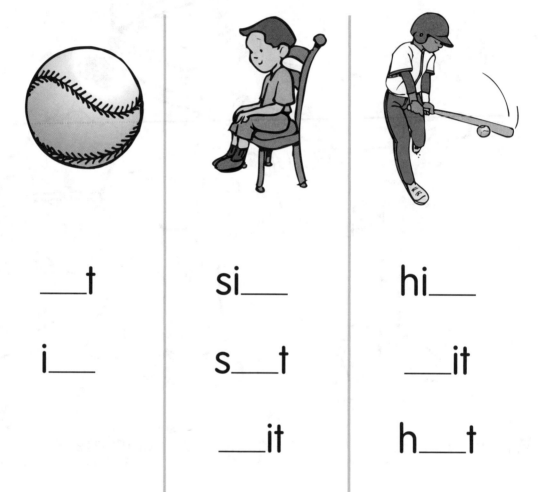

__t   si__   hi__

i__   s__t   __it

                __it   h__t

Write a sentence about a big hit.

_____

_____

It Rhymes with

Write **it** to spell each word.

h ___ ___

s ___ ___ ___

l ___ ___

b ___ ___ ___

Skills:

Auditory
Discrimination

Practicing the
it Family

Skills:

Word Meaning

Using Picture
Clues

Identifying
Like Words

Make a Match

Draw a line to make a match.

hit

sit

it

Circle the word that is the same as the first word.

it	hit	sit	it
sit	sit	it	hit
hit	it	hit	sit

Capital Letters

The first word in a sentence begins with a capital letter.

A boy hit the ball.

Draw a line to make a match.

c   W

w   G

b   C

g   B

Write the capital letter to complete each sentence.

1. w   _____ill Bill hit it?

2. c   _____an Bill run fast?

3. b   _____ill did run fast.

4. g   _____et the bat.

Ann at Bat

Write the missing word to complete each sentence.

it	sit	hit

1. Ann _____ it.

2. Ann hit _____ with a bat.

3. Now Ann will _____ on the bench.

Get a Hit

Look at the picture.

Write the sentence in the correct order.

he	it?	hit	Did

_____

_____

TEST YOUR SKILLS T-Ball

My Spelling Test

Find the correct answer.
Fill in the circle.

1. _____

1. Which word is spelled correctly?

   ○ sut

2. _____
   ○ sit

2. Which word rhymes with **sit**?

3. _____
   ○ fit
   ○ fat

3. Which sentence begins correctly?

   ○ hit the ball.
   ○ Hit the ball.

4. Which sentence begins correctly?

   ○ Can I hit it?
   ○ can I hit it?

Test Your Skills—Record Form

Unit	Test Page	Topic	Test Your Skills Score (5 possible)	Spelling Test Score (10 possible)
1	12	**A Fat Cat**		
2	22	**Pup**		
3	32	**Pin It**		
4	42	**Fun in the Sun**		
5	52	**Red Hen**		
6	62	**Stan and the Man**		
7	72	**A Hot Pot**		
8	82	**A Big Pig**		
9	92	**Bad Sam**		
10	102	**Go to Sleep**		
11	112	**1, 2, 3**		
12	122	**T-Ball**		

Pull-out Spelling Lists

Use these lists to give spelling tests, post on the refrigerator, and for extra practice.

Unit 1 A Fat Cat	Unit 2 Pup	Unit 3 Pin It
1. cat	1. hop	1. in
2. sat	2. top	2. pin
3. mat	3. mop	3. win

Sharpen Your Skills—Spell & Write • EMC 9718 • © Evan-Moor Corp.

Pull-out Spelling Lists

Use these lists to give spelling tests, post on the refrigerator, and for extra practice.

Unit 4 Fun in the Sun	Unit 5 Red Hen	Unit 6 Stan and the Man
1. fun	1. ten	1. can
2. run	2. hen	2. man
3. sun	3. pen	3. ran

Pull-out Spelling Lists

Use these lists to give spelling tests, post on the refrigerator, and for extra practice.

Unit 7 A Hot Pot	Unit 8 A Big Pig	Unit 9 Bad Sam
1. pot	1. pig	1. wet
2. got	2. dig	2. pet
3. hot	3. big	3. get

Pull-out Spelling Lists

Use these lists to give spelling tests, post on the refrigerator, and for extra practice.

Unit 10 Go to Sleep	Unit 11 1, 2, 3	Unit 12 T-Ball
1. bed	1. bug	1. hit
2. red	2. tug	2. sit
3. fed	3. dug	3. it

Answer Key

Page 3

A Fat Cat

A fat cat sat.
A fat cat sat on a mat.

Find It! Read the spelling words.
Check off the words you can find in the story.
☑ cat   ☑ mat   ☑ sat

Page 5

My Spelling Words

Color the cat.

Write the correct word to complete each sentence.

1. The __cat__ sat on a mat.
2. The cat __sat__ on a mat.
3. The cat sat on a __mat__.

mat   sat   cat

Page 6

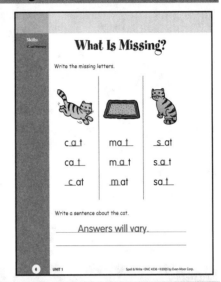

What Is Missing?

Write the missing letters.

c_a_t   m_a_t   _s_at
ca_t_   m_a_t   s_a_t
_c_at   m_a_t   sa_t_

Write a sentence about the cat.

__Answers will vary.__

Page 7

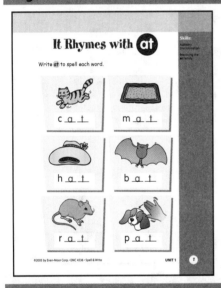

It Rhymes with at

Write **at** to spell each word.

c_a_t   m_a_t

h_a_t   b_a_t

r_a_t   p_a_t

Page 8

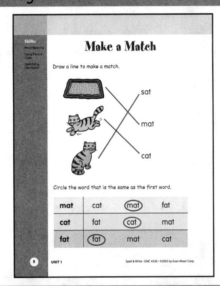

Make a Match

Draw a line to make a match.

sat
mat
cat

Circle the word that is the same as the first word.

mat	cat	(mat)	fat
cat	fat	(cat)	mat
fat	(fat)	mat	cat

Page 9

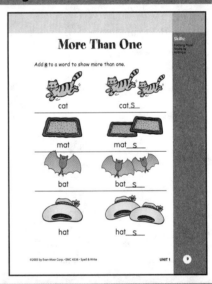

More Than One

Add **s** to a word to show more than one.

cat   cat_s_

mat   mat_s_

bat   bat_s_

hat   hat_s_

Page 10

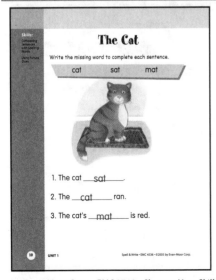

The Cat

Write the missing word to complete each sentence.

cat   sat   mat

1. The cat __sat__.
2. The __cat__ ran.
3. The cat's __mat__ is red.

Page 11

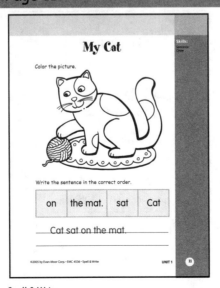

My Cat

Color the picture.

Write the sentence in the correct order.

| on | the mat. | sat | Cat |

__Cat sat on the mat.__

Page 12

SKILLS A Fat Cat

My Spelling Test

Find the correct answer.
Fill in the circle.

1. Which word is spelled correctly?
   ○ kat
   ● cat
2. Which word is spelled correctly?
   ● mat
   ○ mut
3. Which word means more than one bat?
   ● bats
   ○ bat
4. Which word means more than one hat?
   ○ hat
   ● hats

1. _____
2. _____
3. _____

Page 13

Note: Read this story with your child. Ask: What did the puppy spell? Provide any help your child may need to complete the tasks in this unit.

Pup

Did Pup hop?
Pup did hop to the top.
Did Mom mop?
Mom did mop.

Find It! Read the spelling words.
Check off the words you can find in the story.
☑ mop   ☑ hop   ☑ top

©2005 by Evan-Moor Corp. • EMC 4536 • Spell & Write   UNIT 2   13

Page 15

My Spelling Words

Skills:
Visual Discrimination
Letter Order in Words
Comprehension

Color the pup.

Write the correct word to complete each sentence.

Did the pup ___hop___?
The pup did hop on ___top___.
The pup did not ___mop___.

top   hop   mop

©2005 by Evan-Moor Corp. • EMC 4536 • Spell & Write   UNIT 2   15

Page 16

Skills:
Visual Memory

What Is Missing?

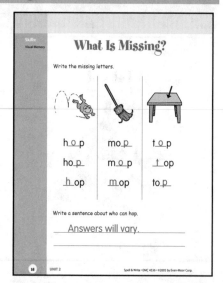

Write the missing letters.

h o p   mo p   t o p
ho p   m o p   t op
h op   mo p   to p

Write a sentence about who can hop.

___Answers will vary.___

16   UNIT 2   Spell & Write • EMC 4536 • ©2005 by Evan-Moor Corp.

Page 17

It Rhymes with **op**

Skills:
Auditory Discrimination
Practicing the op Family

Write **op** to spell each word.

t o p   m o p

p o p   h o p

st o p   sh o p

©2005 by Evan-Moor Corp. • EMC 4536 • Spell & Write   UNIT 2   17

Page 18

Skills:
Word Meaning
Using Picture Clues
Identifying Like Words

Make a Match

Draw a line to make a match.

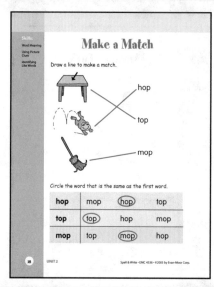

hop
top
mop

Circle the word that is the same as the first word.

hop	mop	(hop)	top
top	(top)	hop	mop
mop	top	(mop)	hop

18   UNIT 2   Spell & Write • EMC 4536 • ©2005 by Evan-Moor Corp.

Page 19

Note: Help your child understand the difference between a sentence that tells something and a sentence that asks a question.

Ask or Tell?

Skills:
Identifying Statements and Questions

Ask: Did the cat hop?
Tell: The cat did hop.

Write a . or a ? to complete each sentence.

1. Did Pup hop _?_
2. Pup did hop _._
3. Mom did mop _._
4. Did Mom mop _?_

Finish the pictures. Draw.

Pup is on top.   Mom did mop.

©2005 by Evan-Moor Corp. • EMC 4536 • Spell & Write   UNIT 2   19

Page 20

Skills:
Completing Sentences with Spelling Words
Using Picture Clues

See Pup

Write the missing word to complete each sentence.

mop   hop   top

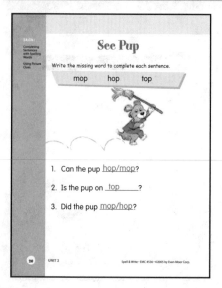

1. Can the pup _hop/mop_?
2. Is the pup on _top_?
3. Did the pup _mop/hop_?

20   UNIT 2   Spell & Write • EMC 4536 • ©2005 by Evan-Moor Corp.

Page 21

A Funny Frog

Skills:
Sentence Order

Look at the picture.

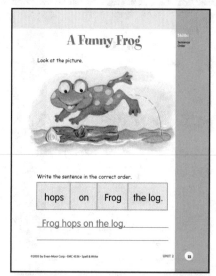

Write the sentence in the correct order.

| hops | on | Frog | the log. |

___Frog hops on the log.___

©2005 by Evan-Moor Corp. • EMC 4536 • Spell & Write   UNIT 2   21

Page 22

Note: Read the questions for your child. Then say each word (mop, top, hop) for your child to write on the spelling test.

TEST YOUR SKILLS Pup

My Spelling Test

Find the correct answer.
Fill in the circle.

1. Which word is spelled correctly?
   ● hop
   ○ hup

2. Which word is spelled correctly?
   ○ mot
   ● mop

3. Does the sentence ask or tell?
   Mom did mop ___
   ● tell
   ○ ask

4. Does the sentence ask or tell?
   Pup did hop ___
   ● tell
   ○ ask

1. ___
2. ___
3. ___

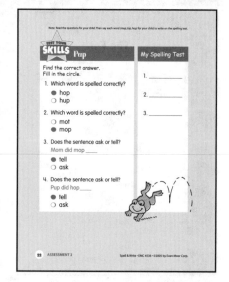

22   ASSESSMENT 2   Spell & Write • EMC 4536 • ©2005 by Evan-Moor Corp.

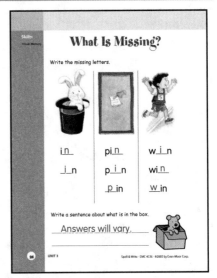

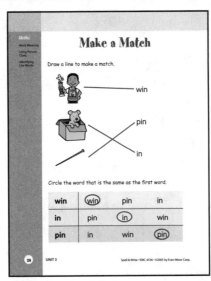

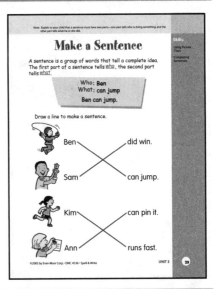

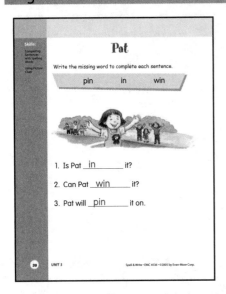

Note: Read this story with your child. Ask What is the girl doing? Provide any help he or she needs to complete the tasks in this unit.

Fun in the Sun

Come run.
Come run in the sun.
It will be fun.

Find It! Read the spelling words.
Check off the words you can find in the story.
✓ run ✓ fun ✓ sun

My Spelling Words

Color the picture.

Write the correct word to complete each sentence.
1. It is ___fun___ to run.
2. It is fun to ___run___.
3. It is fun to run in the ___sun___.

run   fun   sun

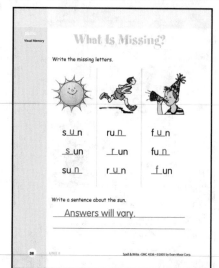

Visual Discrimination
Letter Order in Words
Comprehension

What Is Missing?

Write the missing letters.

s u n   r u n   f u n
s _ un   _ r un   fu _ n
su _ n   r _ un   _ f un

Write a sentence about the sun.
___Answers will vary.___

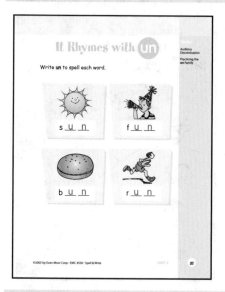

Auditory Discrimination
Practicing the un Family

It Rhymes with un

Write **un** to spell each word.

s u n   f u n
b u n   r u n

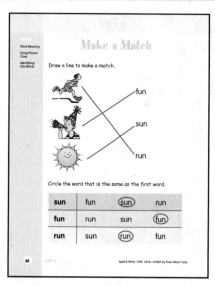

Word Meaning
Using Picture Clues
Identifying Like Words

Make a Match

Draw a line to make a match.

fun
sun
run

Circle the word that is the same as the first word.

sun	fun	(sun)	run
fun	run	sun	(fun)
run	sun	(run)	fun

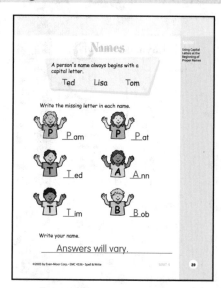

Using Capital Letters at the Beginning of Proper Names

Names

A person's name always begins with a capital letter.

Ted   Lisa   Tom

Write the missing letter in each name.

P _P_am   P _P_at
T _T_ed   A _A_nn
T _T_im   B _B_ob

Write your name.
___Answers will vary.___

Completing Sentences with Spelling Words
Using Picture Clues

Run, Pat, Run

Write the missing word to complete each sentence.

fun   sun   run

1. Pat can ___run___.
2. It is ___fun___ to run in the sun.
3. Pat had fun running in the ___sun___.

Run in the Sun

Look at the picture.

Sentence Order

Write the sentence in the correct order.

| in the sun. | to run | It is | fun |

___It is fun to run in the sun.___

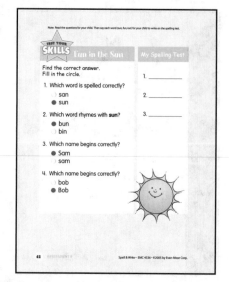

Note: Read the questions for your child. Then say each word (sun, fun, run) for your child to write on the spelling test.

TEST YOUR SKILLS Fun in the Sun   My Spelling Test

Find the correct answer.
Fill in the circle.
1. Which word is spelled correctly?
   ○ san
   ● sun
2. Which word rhymes with **sun**?
   ● bun
   ○ bin
3. Which name begins correctly?
   ● Sam
   ○ sam
4. Which name begins correctly?
   ○ bob
   ● Bob

1. _____
2. _____
3. _____

Red Hen

See the hen.
The hen is in a pen.

See the nest.
See ten eggs in the nest.

Find It! Read the spelling words.
Check off the words you can find in the story.
✓ ten ✓ hen ✓ pen

My Spelling Words

Color the picture.

Write the correct word to complete each sentence.

1. A big __hen__ is in the pen.
2. A big hen is in the __pen__.
3. A big hen sees __ten__.

pen   ten   hen

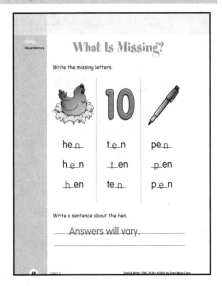

What Is Missing?

Write the missing letters.

10

he_n_   t_e_n   pe_n_
h_e_n   _t_en   _p_en
_h_en   te_n   p_e_n

Write a sentence about the hen.
__Answers will vary.__

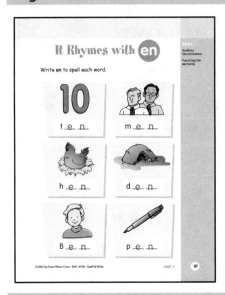

It Rhymes with en

Write en to spell each word.

10
t_en_

m_en_

h_en_

d_en_

B_en_

p_en_

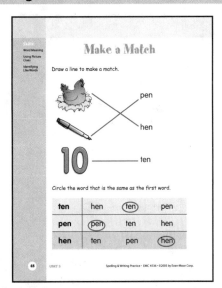

Make a Match

Draw a line to make a match.

pen

hen

10 ——— ten

Circle the word that is the same as the first word.

ten	hen	(ten)	pen
pen	(pen)	ten	hen
hen	ten	pen	(hen)

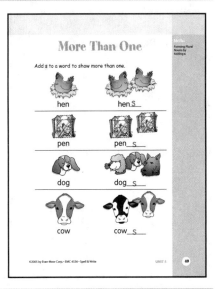

More Than One

Add s to a word to show more than one.

hen   hen_s_

pen   pen_s_

dog   dog_s_

cow   cow_s_

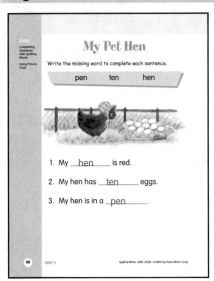

My Pet Hen

Write the missing word to complete each sentence.

pen   ten   hen

1. My __hen__ is red.
2. My hen has __ten__ eggs.
3. My hen is in a __pen__.

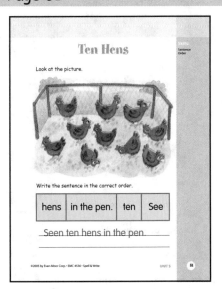

Ten Hens

Look at the picture.

Write the sentence in the correct order.

| hens | in the pen. | ten | See |

__Seen ten hens in the pen.__

TEST YOUR SKILLS   **Red Hen**

My Spelling Test

Find the correct answer.
Fill in the circle.

1. Which word is spelled correctly?
   ○ hin
   ● hen

2. Does **hen** rhyme with **pen**?
   ● yes
   ○ no

3. Which word means more than one hen?
   ● hens
   ○ hen

4. Which word means more than one den?
   ○ den
   ● dens

1. _____
2. _____
3. _____

Page 53

Stan and the Man

Stan got the can.
Stan ran.

Can the man get Stan?
Yes, he can.

Find It! Read the spelling words.
Check off the words you can find in the story.

✓ can   ✓ man   ✓ ran

Page 55

My Spelling Words

Color the picture.

Write the correct word to complete each sentence.

1. The man had a _can_.
2. The dog _ran_ to the man.
3. The _man_ fed the dog.

can   ran   man

Page 56

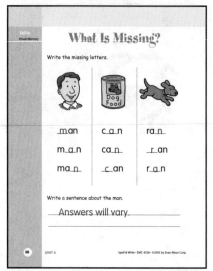

What Is Missing?

Write the missing letters.

man	_c a n_	_ra n_
_m a n_	_ca n_	_r a n_
_ma n_	_c a n_	_r a n_

Write a sentence about the man.

Answers will vary.

Page 57

It Rhymes with an

Write an to spell each word.

_c a n_   _m a n_

_v a n_   _p a n_

_St a n_   _f a n_

Page 58

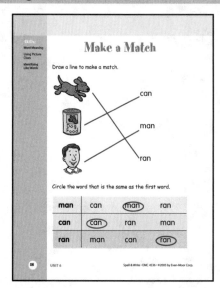

Make a Match

Draw a line to make a match.

can
man
ran

Circle the word that is the same as the first word.

man	can	(man)	ran
can	(can)	ran	man
ran	man	can	(ran)

Page 59

Ask or Tell?

Ask: Did the man run?
Tell: The man did run.

Write a . or a ? to complete each sentence.

1. Did the man get Stan _?_
2. Did the dog run _?_
3. The man fed Stan _._
4. Stan is a dog _._

Draw.

| The dog ran. | The man did _not_ run. |

Page 60

Stan Ran

Write the missing word to complete each sentence.

Stan   man   ran   can

1. Stan _ran_.
2. The _man_ ran to get Stan.
3. The man got a _can_.
4. The man fed _Stan_.

Page 61

Dan's Pups

Look at the picture.

Write the sentence in the correct order.

| ran | to the can. | The pups |

The pups ran to the can.

Page 62

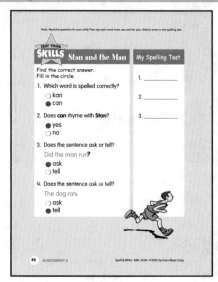

SKILLS Stan and the Man   My Spelling Test

Find the correct answer.
Fill in the circle.

1. Which word is spelled correctly?
   ○ kan
   ● can

2. Does **can** rhyme with **Stan**?
   ● yes
   ○ no

3. Does the sentence ask or tell?
   Did the man run?
   ● ask
   ○ tell

4. Does the sentence ask or tell?
   The dog ran.
   ○ ask
   ● tell

1. _____
2. _____
3. _____

Page 63

A Hot Pot

Is the pot hot?
It is hot.
Dad got the hot pot.

Find It! Read the spelling words.
Check off the words you can find in the story.
☑ pot   ☑ got   ☑ hot

Page 65

My Spelling Words

Color the picture.

Write the correct word to complete each sentence.

1. Did Dad get the ___pot___ ?
2. Dad ___got___ the pot.
3. The pot is not ___hot___ .

got   hot   pot

Page 66

What Is Missing?

Write the missing letters.

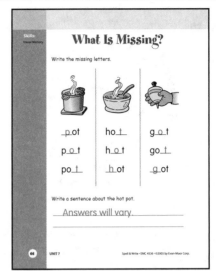

_p_ot   ho_t_   _g_ot
p_o_t   h_o_t   go_t_
po_t_   _h_ot   _g_ot

Write a sentence about the hot pot.

___Answers will vary.___

Page 67

It Rhymes with ot

Write **ot** to spell each word.

p_o_t   h_o_t

c_o_t   d_o_t

Page 68

Make a Match

Draw a line to make a match.

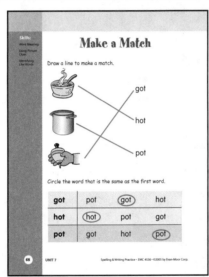

got
hot
pot

Circle the word that is the same as the first word.

got	pot	(got)	hot
hot	(hot)	pot	got
pot	got	hot	(pot)

Page 69

Capital Letters

The first word in a sentence
begins with a capital letter.
The pot is hot.

Draw a line to make a match.

n   T
p   N
t   P

Write the capital letter to complete each sentence.

1. p   _P_ut it in the pot.
2. t   _T_he pot is hot.
3. n   _N_an got the pot.

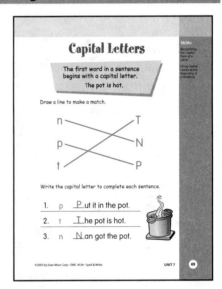

Page 70

Kim

Write the missing word to complete each sentence.

hot   got   pot

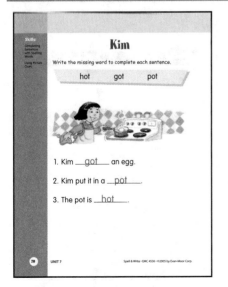

1. Kim ___got___ an egg.
2. Kim put it in a ___pot___ .
3. The pot is ___hot___ .

Page 71

It Is Hot!

Look at the picture.

Write the sentence in the correct order.

| the hot pot. | got | The man |

___The man got the hot pot.___

Page 72

TEST YOUR SKILLS A Hot Pot

Find the correct answer.
Fill in the circle.

1. Which word is spelled correctly?
   ○ het
   ● hot

2. Is the pot hot?
   ● yes
   ○ no

3. Which sentence begins correctly?
   ○ dad got it.
   ● Dad got it.

4. Which sentence begins correctly?
   ● Get the pot.
   ○ get the pot.

My Spelling Test

1. _____
2. _____
3. _____

Page 73

Note: Read this story with your child. Ask: *What did the pig dig up?* Provide any help he or she needs to complete the tasks in this unit.

A Big Pig

See the big pig.
See the pig dig.

Stop, pig, stop!
Do not dig!

Find It! Read the spelling words.
Check off the words you can find in the story.

☑ pig ☑ dig ☑ big

©2005 by Evan-Moor Corp. • EMC 4536 • Spell & Write   UNIT 8   73

Page 75

My Spelling Words

Color the picture.

Write the correct word to complete each sentence.

1. See the big ___pig___ dig in the mud.
2. See the ___big___ pig dig in the mud.
3. See the big pig ___dig___ in the mud.

dig   pig   big

©2005 by Evan-Moor Corp. • EMC 4536 • Spell & Write   UNIT 8   75

Page 76

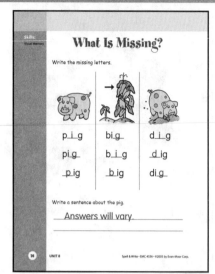

Skills: Visual Memory

What Is Missing?

Write the missing letters.

p i g   b i g   d i g
pi g   b i g   d ig
p i g   b i g   di g

Write a sentence about the pig.

___Answers will vary.___

76   UNIT 8   Spell & Write • EMC 4536 • ©2005 by Evan-Moor Corp.

Page 77

It Rhymes with ig

Skills: Auditory Discrimination / Practicing the ig Word Family

Write ig to spell each word.

p i g   d i g
w i g   tw i g
b i g   f i g

©2005 by Evan-Moor Corp. • EMC 4536 • Spell & Write   UNIT 8   77

Page 78

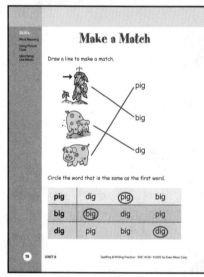

Skills: Word Meaning / Using Picture Clues / Identifying Like Words

Make a Match

Draw a line to make a match.

pig
big
dig

Circle the word that is the same as the first word.

pig	dig	(pig)	big
big	(big)	dig	pig
dig	pig	big	(dig)

78   UNIT 8   Spelling & Writing Practice • EMC 4536 • ©2005 by Evan-Moor Corp.

Page 79

Name the Pigs

Skills: Beginning Proper Names with a Capital Letter

Write the missing letter to spell each pig's name.

B   D   J   P   S

b B en   s S am
d D an   p P am
j J ane   j J ill

Write your name.

___Answers will vary.___

©2005 by Evan-Moor Corp. • EMC 4536 • Spell & Write   UNIT 8   79

Page 80

Skills: Completing Sentences with Spelling Words / Using Picture Clues

Pet Pig

Write the missing word to complete each sentence.

dig   pig   big

1. My pet pig is ___big___.
2. My pet pig can ___dig___.
3. My pet ___pig___ can run.

80   UNIT 8   Spell & Write • EMC 4536 • ©2005 by Evan-Moor Corp.

Page 81

Skills: Sentence Order

In the Pigpen

Look at the picture.

Write the sentence in the correct order.

| the big pig | dig? | Did |

___Did the big pig dig?___

©2005 by Evan-Moor Corp. • EMC 4536 • Spell & Write   UNIT 8   81

Page 82

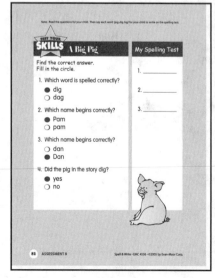

TEST YOUR SKILLS A Big Pig

Find the correct answer.
Fill in the circle.

1. Which word is spelled correctly?
   ● dig
   ○ dag

2. Which name begins correctly?
   ● Pam
   ○ pam

3. Which name begins correctly?
   ○ dan
   ● Dan

4. Did the pig in the story dig?
   ● yes
   ○ no

My Spelling Test

1. _____
2. _____
3. _____

82   ASSESSMENT 8   Spell & Write • EMC 4536 • ©2005 by Evan-Moor Corp.

140

Sharpen Your Skills—Spell & Write • EMC 9718 • © Evan-Moor Corp.

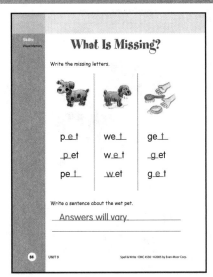

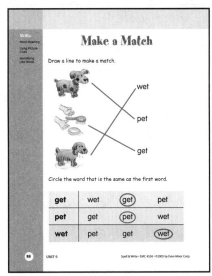

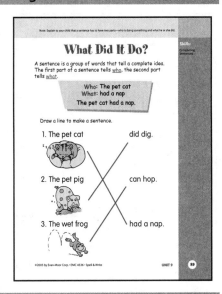

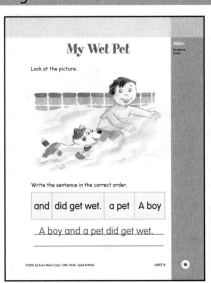

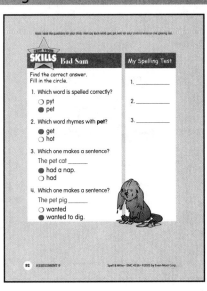

Page 93

Go to Sleep

Fred is fed.
It is time for bed.
Fred's bed is red.

Find It! Read the spelling words.
Check off the words you can find in the story.

☑ bed   ☑ red   ☑ fed

©2005 by Evan-Moor Corp. • EMC 4536 • Spell & Write   UNIT 10   93

Page 95

My Spelling Words

Visual Discrimination
Letter Order in Words
Comprehension

Color the picture.

Write the correct word to complete each sentence.

1. Fred was __fed__.

2. Fred is in __bed__.

3. Fred is in his __red__ bed.

bed   fed   red

©2005 by Evan-Moor Corp. • EMC 4536 • Spell & Write   UNIT 10   95

Page 96

Visual Memory

What Is Missing?

Write the missing letters.

b e d   fe d   r e d

b ed   f e d   r ed

be d   f ed   re d

Write a sentence about the red bed.

__Answers will vary.__

96   UNIT 10   Spell & Write • EMC 4536 • ©2005 by Evan-Moor Corp.

Page 97

It Rhymes with **ed**

Auditory Discrimination
Practicing the ed Family

Write **ed** to spell each word.

b e d   f e d

r e d   w e d

T e d   sh e d

©2005 by Evan-Moor Corp. • EMC 4536 • Spell & Write   UNIT 10   97

Page 98

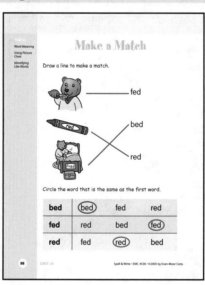

Word Meaning
Using Picture Clues
Identifying Like Words

Make a Match

Draw a line to make a match.

fed

bed

red

Circle the word that is the same as the first word.

bed	(bed)	fed	red
fed	red	bed	(fed)
red	fed	(red)	bed

98   UNIT 10   Spell & Write • EMC 4536 • ©2005 by Evan-Moor Corp.

Page 99

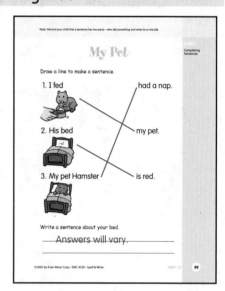

Note: Remind your child that a sentence has two parts—who did something and what he or she did.

My Pet

Completing Sentences

Draw a line to make a sentence.

1. I fed   had a nap.

2. His bed   my pet.

3. My pet Hamster   is red.

Write a sentence about your bed.

__Answers will vary.__

©2005 by Evan-Moor Corp. • EMC 4536 • Spell & Write   UNIT 10   99

Page 100

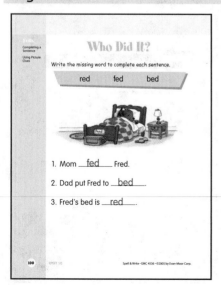

Completing a Sentence
Using Picture Clues

Who Did It?

Write the missing word to complete each sentence.

red   fed   bed

1. Mom __fed__ Fred.

2. Dad put Fred to __bed__.

3. Fred's bed is __red__.

100   UNIT 10   Spell & Write • EMC 4536 • ©2005 by Evan-Moor Corp.

Page 101

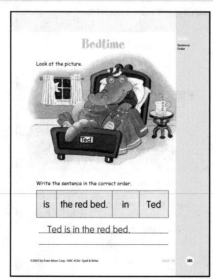

Bedtime

Sentence Order

Look at the picture.

Write the sentence in the correct order.

is	the red bed.	in	Ted

__Ted is in the red bed.__

©2005 by Evan-Moor Corp. • EMC 4536 • Spell & Write   UNIT 10   101

Page 102

Note: Read the questions for your child. Then say each spelling word (fed, bed, red) for your child to write on the spelling test.

TEST YOUR SKILLS   Go to Sleep   My Spelling Test

Find the correct answer.
Fill in the circle.

1. Which word is spelled correctly?
   ● bed
   ○ bede

2. Which word rhymes with **Fred**?
   ● bed
   ○ bad

3. What color was Fred's bed?
   ○ green
   ● red

4. Which one makes a sentence?
   Teddy is _____
   ● in the bed.
   ○ in the

1. _____

2. _____

3. _____

102   ASSESSMENT 10   Spell & Write • EMC 4536 • ©2005 by Evan-Moor Corp.

Page 103

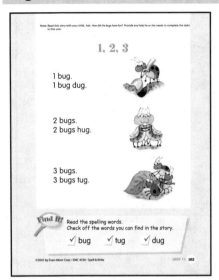

Note: Read this story with your child. Ask: How did the bugs have fun? Provide any help he or she needs to complete the tasks in this unit.

1, 2, 3

1 bug.
1 bug dug.

2 bugs.
2 bugs hug.

3 bugs.
3 bugs tug.

Find It! Read the spelling words.
Check off the words you can find in the story.
✓ bug   ✓ tug   ✓ dug

©2005 by Evan-Moor Corp. • EMC 4536 • Spell & Write   UNIT 11   103

Page 105

My Spelling Words

Skills:
Visual Discrimination
Letter Order in Words
Comprehension

Color the picture.

Write the correct word to complete each sentence.

1. Ann __dug__ it up.
2. Ann had to __tug__ on the box.
3. A __bug__ is on the box.

bug   tug   dug

©2005 by Evan-Moor • EMC 4536 • Spell & Write   UNIT 11   105

Page 106

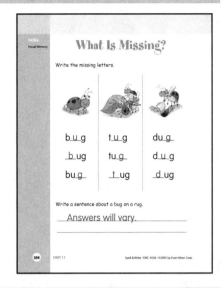

Skills:
Visual Memory

What Is Missing?

Write the missing letters.

b_u_g   t_u_g   du_g_
_b_ug   tug   _d_ug
bu_g_   _t_ug   _d_ug

Write a sentence about a bug on a rug.

__Answers will vary.__

106   UNIT 11   Spell & Write • EMC 4536 • ©2005 by Evan-Moor Corp.

Page 107

It Rhymes with (ug)

Skills:
Auditory Discrimination
Practicing the -ug Family

Write **ug** to spell each word.

b_u_g   r_u_g

m_u_g   t_u_g

h_u_g   pl_u_g

©2005 by Evan-Moor Corp. • EMC 4536 • Spelling & Writing Practice   UNIT 11   107

Page 108

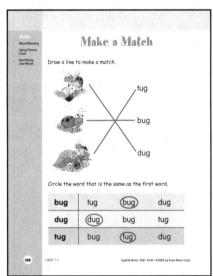

Skills:
Word Meaning
Using Picture Clues
Identifying Like Words

Make a Match

Draw a line to make a match.

tug

bug

dug

Circle the word that is the same as the first word.

bug	tug	(bug)	dug
dug	(dug)	bug	tug
tug	bug	(tug)	dug

108   UNIT 11   Spell & Write • EMC 4536 • ©2005 by Evan-Moor Corp.

Page 109

More Than One

Skills:
Forming Plural Nouns by Adding s

Add **s** to a word to show more than one.
bug   bugs

Look at the picture. Write the correct word.

bug	bug_s_
dog	dog_s_
mug	mug_s_

©2005 by Evan-Moor Corp. • EMC 4536 • Spelling & Writing Practice   UNIT 11   109

Page 110

Skills:
Completing Sentences with Spelling Words
Using Picture Clues

A Bug

Write the missing word to complete each sentence.

hug   tug   bug

1. Will the __bug__ tug?
2. The bug will __tug__.
3. The bug will not __hug__.

UNIT 11   Spell & Write • EMC 4536 • ©2005 by Evan-Moor Corp.

Page 111

Bug Fun

Skills:
Sentence Order

Look at the picture.

Write the sentence in the correct order.

| dug | a fat bug. | up | Pat |

__Pat dug up a fat bug.__

©2005 by Evan-Moor Corp. • EMC 4536 • Spell & Write   UNIT 11   111

Page 112

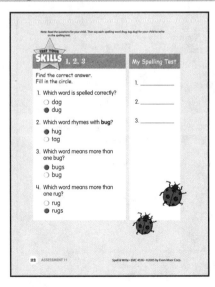

Note: Read the questions for your child. Then say each spelling word (bug, tug, dug) for your child to write on the spelling test.

TEST YOUR SKILLS 1, 2, 3

Find the correct answer.
Fill in the circle.

1. Which word is spelled correctly?
   ○ dag
   ● dug

2. Which word rhymes with **bug**?
   ● hug
   ○ tag

3. Which word means more than one bug?
   ● bugs
   ○ bug

4. Which word means more than one rug?
   ○ rug
   ● rugs

My Spelling Test

1. _____
2. _____
3. _____

112   ASSESSMENT 11   Spell & Write • EMC 4536 • ©2005 by Evan-Moor Corp.

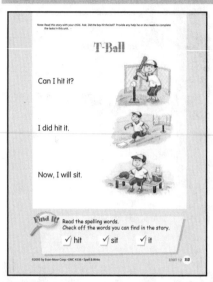

T-Ball

Can I hit it?

I did hit it.

Now, I will sit.

Find It! Read the spelling words.
Check off the words you can find in the story.

✓ hit   ✓ sit   ✓ it

My Spelling Words

Color the picture.

Write the correct word to complete each sentence.

1. Did she __hit__ it?
2. She did hit __it__.
3. Will she __sit__ or run?

it   hit   sit

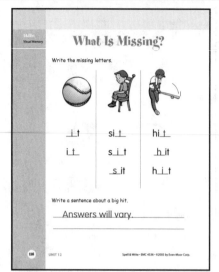

What Is Missing?

Write the missing letters.

_it   si_t   hi_t
_it   s_it   _hit
    _s it   h_it

Write a sentence about a big hit.

__Answers will vary.__

It Rhymes with it

Write it to spell each word.

h_it   s_it
l_it   b_it

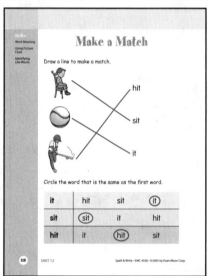

Make a Match

Draw a line to make a match.

hit
sit
it

Circle the word that is the same as the first word.

it	hit	sit	(it)
sit	(sit)	it	hit
hit	it	(hit)	sit

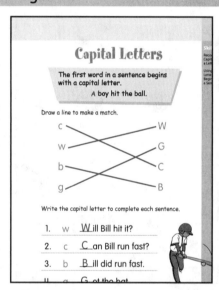

Capital Letters

The first word in a sentence begins
with a capital letter.
A boy hit the ball.

Draw a line to make a match.

c   W
w   G
b   C
g   B

Write the capital letter to complete each sentence.

1. w   __W__ill Bill hit it?
2. c   __C__an Bill run fast?
3. b   __B__ill did run fast.
4. g   __G__ot the bat.

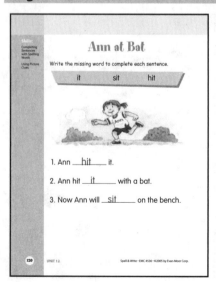

Ann at Bat

Write the missing word to complete each sentence.

it   sit   hit

1. Ann __hit__ it.
2. Ann hit __it__ with a bat.
3. Now Ann will __sit__ on the bench.

Get a Hit

Look at the picture.

Write the sentence in the correct order.

| he | it? | hit | Did |

__Did he hit it?__

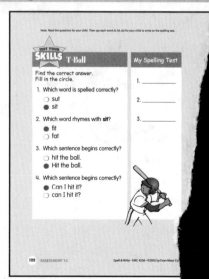

SKILLS T-Ball

Find the correct answer.
Fill in the circle.

1. Which word is spelled correctly?
   ○ sut
   ● sit
2. Which word rhymes with **sit**?
   ● fit
   ○ fat
3. Which sentence begins correctly?
   ○ hit the ball.
   ● Hit the ball.
4. Which sentence begins correctly?
   ● Can I hit it?
   ○ can I hit it?

My Spelling Test

1. _____
2. _____
3. _____